T0340316

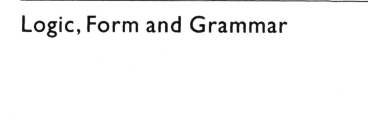

Logic, Form and Grammar

International Library of Philosophy

Edited by José Bermúdez, Tim Crane and Peter Sullivan

Advisory Board: Jonathan Barnes, Fred Dretske, Frances Kamm, Brian Leiter, Huw Price, Sydney Shoemaker

Logic, Form and Grammar

Peter Long

Routledge
Taylor & Francis Group

LONDON AND NEW YORK

First published 2001
by Routledge
2 Park Square, Milton Park, Abingdon, Oxon, OX14 4RN

Simultaneously published in the USA and Canada
by Routledge
605 Third Avenue, New York, NY 10017

Routledge is an imprint of the Taylor & Francis Group, an informa business

© 2001 Peter Long

Typeset in Times by
RefineCatch Limited, Bungay, Suffolk

British Library Cataloguing in Publication Data
A catalogue record for this book is available from the British Library

Library of Congress Cataloging in Publication Data
Long, Peter, 1926–
    Logic, form, and grammar / Peter Long.
        p. cm. – (International library of philosophy)
    Includes bibliographical references (p.) and index.
    1. Form (Logic) I. Title. II. Series.
    BC199.F6 L66   2001
    160–dc21   00–055322

ISBN13: 978-0-415-24224-0 (hbk)
ISBN13: 978-0-4154-0808-0 (pbk)

For my father and mother

Wer nicht weiterdenkt, denkt überhaupt nicht.
(Schnitzler)

Contents

Acknowledgements

I am grateful to the Editor of *The Philosophical Quarterly* for permission to reprint 'Formal Relations', which appeared in that journal in April 1982, and to Kluwer academic publishers for permission to reprint 'Universals: Logic and Metaphor', which appeared in volume 17 of the Nijhoff International Philosophy Series, entitled *Philosophy and Life* (1984, The Hague).

It gives me pleasure to record my debt to Peter Sullivan for having drawn my attention to some errors in an earlier draft of 'Logical Form and Hypothetical Reasoning' and for suggesting certain improvements in the development of the argument.

Introduction

Common to the three essays printed here is a preoccupation with the notion of logical form, and, thereby, with that of a formal relation.

In the last two essays, where the concern is primarily with the notion of logical form as it applies to *propositions*, the formal relation is a relation internal to propositions. Thus we speak of the relation of a thing's having a property (of an object's falling under a concept) or of the relation of a relation's relating its terms, and here the relation is one that is expressed in a proposition through its being of the form *Fa* or *Fab* and so on. The confusion of such formal relations with relations proper – relations for which there exists or could exist an expression in the language – is common in philosophy and appears at its most blatant in Locke's theory of a substratum or property-less subject of properties and Bradley's polemic against relations, where he asserts that a relation has to be related to its terms in order to relate them. The confusion is at the root of the theory that properties and relations are universals and is responsible for the assimilation of facts to complexes, which is found in the early pages of the *Tractatus*.

In the first, major, essay, the concern is primarily with the notion of logical form as it applies to *arguments*, and here the formal relation is a relation between propositions. Thus in the syllogism 'Every Athenian is Greek; Socrates is an Athenian: therefore Socrates is Greek', the third proposition is inferable from the first two in that they are respectively of the forms *Ga*, *every F is G*, *Fa*, or, as we may put it, in that the first two stand to the third in the relation *every F is G*, *Fa : Ga*. The propositions standing in this relation are all asserted in the syllogism, but it is not hard to show that an argument in which not all three propositions are asserted may have the same logical form as the syllogism. An example would be 'Every Athenian is Greek: therefore if Socrates is an Athenian then he is Greek', in which the conclusion is a hypothetical statement, so that only one of the three propositions is asserted. We thus arrive at the concept of a *hypothetical variant* of an argument – a concept which is indispensable for understanding the role of hypotheticals in inference, whether as premisses or conclusion.

A classic example of such is a *modus ponens*, in which the consequent of a hypothetical is inferred from it together with its antecedent. No argument could be simpler than 'If Socrates is an Athenian then Socrates is Greek; Socrates is an Athenian: therefore Socrates is Greek', and it is evident that it is valid in virtue of its form alone, irrespective of subject matter. It is therefore surprising that logic, as the science of formally valid inference, has failed to make good the claim that an argument by *modus ponens* belongs to logic – has failed to make it good in the only way that is possible: by demonstrating that the *principle* under which we draw inferences when we execute a *modus ponens* is a principle of logic.

If we ask how it is possible that, notwithstanding the advanced state of the subject, no such demonstration should have been given, the answer must lie in the failure to recognise that the notion of the form of an argument – as when we speak of 'the form under which an argument is valid' – is not one indivisible notion. This can be seen from the case of the argument with the hypothetical conclusion. As a dialectical structure, this is a distinct form of argument from the syllogism and yet, as a hypothetical variant of the syllogism, it enjoys the same principle, *viz.* 'If every *F* is *G* and if *Fa* then *Ga*'. We thus have a distinction between the form under which an argument is valid as a piece of reasoning in which an inference is drawn from such and such a premiss or premisses to such and such a conclusion, which we call its *argument form*, and the form as determined by the principle of the argument, which we call its *root form*. Accordingly, where the principle is one that belongs to logic, as it is here, root form is the same as logical form.

Furnished with this distinction and the notion of a hypothetical variant, it becomes possible for the first time to command a clear view of the role of hypothetical statements in inference and to articulate the principles of formally valid arguments that contain such statements. In the case of an argument in which premisses and conclusion are *simply assertoric* – statements in which a *proposition* (expression for a truth-value) is put forward as true – neglect of the distinction causes no harm, since it can be shown that here argument form and root form coincide. However, in the case of an argument in which premisses or conclusion are hypotheticals, where argument form and root form are distinct, it will perhaps be appreciated why logicians, who have hitherto proceeded dogmatically and not called in question the notion of *the* form under which an argument is valid, should have even failed to make good the claim that such a simple argument as a *modus ponens* belongs to logic. Or failing this, to show reason why – its formal validity notwithstanding – it does not.

There is perhaps no chapter in the history of logic so beset with difficulties as that concerning arguments in which hypotheticals figure. In the present essay these difficulties are finally resolved and the status of any formally valid argument in which hypothetical statements occur essentially is determined. In particular, we have a resolution of the paradox from which the argument of the essay takes its beginning: *How can logic make good its claim to be the theory of formal inference when the form under which an argument by* modus ponens *is valid – the form represented by the schema 'If p then q; p: therefore q' – does not represent a logical form?*

Logical form and hypothetical reasoning

Synopsis

1. Logic is the science of formal inference. Hence an argument by *modus ponens*, in which the consequent of a hypothetical is inferred from it together with its antecedent(s), should be one whose form belongs to logic.

2. But there is no difference in *logical form* between the argument 'Either Eliot or Yeats died before 1940; Eliot did not die before that date: therefore Yeats did' and the argument 'Either E or Y; therefore if not-E then Y'. So the particle forming a hypothetical is not a logical constant. It thus appears that the form of a *modus ponens* – the form represented by the schema 'If p then q; p: therefore q' – is not a logical form. So how *can* logic be the science of formal inference?

3. The recognition that arguments so related have the same logical form is almost immediate once it is acknowledged that the logical form of an argument is independent of whether its limbs – the propositions upon whose forms its validity depends – are asserted.

4. Here it may be objected that since an argument must conclude with an assertion, its limbs must all be asserted. But this is to assume that the conclusion of an argument can only be a statement asserting a proposition and a hypothetical is not of this kind. With a hypothetical it is the mode of assertion that is complex, not a propositional content. A statement whose mode of assertion consists in putting a proposition, an expression for a truth-value, forward as true, may be called *simply assertoric*.

5. We represent a (singular) hypothetical as having the form 'If $p_1, \ldots, p_n$ then q', from which it can be seen that the subordinate clause(s) of such a statement lie outside the scope of the main verb. So the form of the subordinate clause(s) must bear on the linguistic act effected by its utterance, in which case such a statement is not simply assertoric.

6. A sign only determines a logical form together with its 'logico-syntactic

employment'. Thus the statement 'If Black is in need of another drink, there is some wine left in the decanter' does not count as a hypothetical because it cannot be validly contraposed and the conditional prediction 'If the wind drops, it will rain' does not count as such because the subordinate clause lies *within* the scope of the main verb.

7. Refutation of von Wright's view of hypotheticals. A hypothetical can be characterised as a statement in which one proposition is asserted on the condition of the truth of another, but this is not to say that in uttering such a statement you are effecting a conditional act. On the understanding of 'condition'.

8. The hypothetical form does not only comprehend statements in the indicative mood. The significance of couching a hypothetical in the subjunctive mood.

9. In which it is shown that corresponding arguments of the forms *p, q: therefore r* and *p: therefore if q then r* have the same logical form.

10. The same is true of corresponding arguments of the forms *p, q: therefore r* and *p: therefore since q, r*. The conclusion of an argument of this second form, in which the antecedent is introduced as a *thesis*, we call a *thetical* statement.

11. We are thus brought to acknowledge the concept of a *dialectical variant* of an argument. An argument of the form *p: therefore if q then r* we call a *hypothetical variant* of the corresponding argument with two premisses, and one of the form *p: therefore since q, r* we call a *thetical variant*. The notion of a degenerate variant.

12. An argument whose premisses and conclusion are simply assertoric we call a *standard* argument. A standard argument will then have $2^n - 1$ (hypo) thetical variants, where *n* is the number of premisses. Whilst the classical definition of a valid argument is framed only for standard arguments, it does not need supplementing to provide for the case of a dialectical variant. The validity of a variant reduces to the validity of the argument of which it is a variant.

13. Why not all hypothetical variants of a disjunctive syllogism can be couched in the subjunctive form.

14. The idiomatic use of the hypothetical form explained.

15. Criticism of Quine's defence of the analysis of (indicative) hypotheticals as material conditionals.

16. With the concept of a dialectical variant it is borne upon us that different forms of argument can all share the same logical form. Thus 'the form under which the argument . . . is valid' may allude either to what we shall call the *argument form* of an argument, which is different in an argument and its dialectical variants, or to what we shall call the *root form*, which is common to an argument and its variants. Logical form is a special case of root form.

17. The argument form is the form under which an argument is valid *as an inference from such and such premisses to such and such a conclusion*. As such it will often be represented by a schema of the argument and it can always be so represented if the argument is a standard one. However, the argument form of a dialectical variant cannot be so represented.

18. In which it is shown that the argument form of a hypothetical variant cannot be represented by an argument schema. A hypothetical statement is *dialectically ambiguous*: how it is to be read depends on the variant of which it is to be seen as the conclusion.

19. It follows that the argument form of a hypothetical variant can only be given by reference to the form of the argument of which it is a variant.

20. If an argument has a hypothetical premiss as well as a hypothetical conclusion then the concept of a hypothetical variant enters twice over in the description of its argument form. Argument by contraposition and the hypothetical syllogism.

21. Criticism of Frege's remark in the *Begriffsschrift* that a causal connection is contained in the word 'if'.

22. The difficulties encountered by logicians in understanding the relationship of hypothetical statements to truth-functional ones have their resolution in the concept of a hypothetical variant.

23. The root form of an argument is determined by its principle. If the principle is one that belongs to logic, the root form will be a logical form. The root form of a standard argument is the same as its argument form.

24. An explanation is needed how different *forms of argument* – arguments as different as a disjunctive syllogism and its various dialectical variants – can have the same root form. The explanation is to be found in the *distributive* character of the concept of a *ground*.

25. In a thetical statement the consequent is asserted on the ground of the truth of the antecedent(s). To understand how such a statement is then

distinguished from the corresponding argument, we have to distinguish two ways of construing 'asserting Q on the ground of the truth of P', according to whether the verb has wide or narrow scope.

26. It is essential to the notion of a ground that if the truth of P and Q serve as a ground for asserting R then the truth of P serves as a ground for asserting R on the ground of the truth of Q. This explains how it is possible that an argument should have thetical variants.

27. In a hypothetical the consequent is asserted on the potential ground of the truth of the antecedent(s). But again, if the truth of P and Q serve as a ground for asserting R then the truth of P serves as a ground for asserting R on the potential ground of the truth of Q. This explains how it is possible that an argument should have hypothetical variants.

28. To win recognition for the notion of asserting one proposition on the potential ground of the truth of another, we need to understand how the grammatical make-up of a hypothetical bears upon the linguistic act effected by its utterance.

29. The concept of the *Mood* of a sentence as that property of a sentence which identifies the act effected by its utterance. We distinguish between Mood and the *mark* by which it is conveyed.

30. The (simple) assertoric Mood is related to what Frege calls 'assertoric force', but Frege's concept sins against his dictum 'always to separate sharply the psychological from the logical'.

31. Recognition of a sentence as a formation to which a Mood is essential underlies the distinction between sentence and clause. With his assertion-sign Frege constructed a sentence that is not formed by a grammatical clause.

32. Contrary to the *Tractatus* view, it is not the likeness of a propositional sign to the printed word that made it possible for Frege to construe a proposition as a complex name, but the fact that no Mood belongs to a proposition *as such*. This also explains why Wittgenstein is able to present his rival account of a proposition as a picture or model of reality.

33. Although no Mood belongs to a proposition as such, we cannot deny a Mood to it when it is a main clause. This will hardly be disputed when it is a main clause that forms a sentence, but it is no less true when it is the main clause *of* a sentence.

34. The consequent of a hypothetical is no exception, even though it is not

asserted. For whether a proposition occurring as the main clause of a sentence is asserted or not must depend on the (complex) Mood of the sentence containing it.

35. The Mood of a sentence of the form *Sub* $p_1, \ldots, p_n, q$ – where 'sub' stands in for a subordinating conjunction – is φ-*wise assertoric*, with the value of 'φ' depending on the particular conjunction by which the sentence is generated. A conjunction that helps to convey the Mood of sentences formed by its means might be called a *conjunction of Mood*.

36. There are conjunctions of Mood in which the conjoined clauses are *co-ordinate* with one another. Here each clause counts as a main clause, the ones preceding the conjunction because they form sentences and the clause following because it is introduced by such a conjunction.

37. The clauses of a truth-functional statement are not bona fide main clauses, and should be thought of as co-ordinate clauses in *one* main clause. On the distinction between 'and' and 'but'.

38. Since the conjunction generating a hypothetical is a conjunction of Mood, a clause that forms a hypothetical, unlike one that forms a sentence that is simply assertoric, cannot occur 'unasserted' in ordinary speech. Having a Mood that is thus *inalienable*, it cannot occur within the scope of a truth-functional connective.

39. On Frege's reading of the conditional stroke in formulas of his *Begriffsschrift*.

40. It follows from §38 that a hypothetical running 'If p then if q then r' has two antecedents, not one. Lewis Carroll's paradox of the barber shop.

41. There may be a point in framing a hypothetical that has multiple antecedents with these arranged stepwise rather than in co-ordination, as we can see if we consider how the hypothetical form of statement might be used in reading proofs in natural deduction format. With this reading it stands out how proof by natural deduction conforms to the ideal of proof *in* logic.

42. On the difference between the formalisation of logic proposed by Gentzen and and the formalisation found in Frege's *Begriffsschrift*.

43. It is not the case that to every valid sequent of propositional logic there corresponds a *principle* of inference. What we call such gives expression to forms under which a proposition Q is inferable from propositions $P_1, \ldots, P_n$

through giving expression to forms under which the truth of $P_1, \ldots, P_n$ would *serve as a ground* for asserting Q.

44. The notion of asserting one proposition on the ground of the truth of another can be taken in two ways according to whether the ground is a ground simpliciter or one 'relative to the subject'. In a hypothetical inferred from a truth-functional premiss the antecedent is introduced only as a proposition whose truth would *serve the speaker* as a ground for asserting the consequent. Such a hypothetical we may call *material*.

45. Where the antecedent is introduced as a proposition whose truth would serve as a ground simpliciter for asserting the consequent, there is always the question of the *form or aspect* under which it is so introduced. In many cases it is so introduced in virtue of bearing a formal relation to the consequent – a relation which requires for its expression propositional letters or letters for names, predicates, relations.

46. Outline of a procedure for determining the formal relation, if any, involved in asserting a given hypothetical.

47. Limitations of the procedure: why it will not serve to determine whether an arbitrary hypothetical is material or not.

48. The *same* antecedent may enter *different* hypotheticals under different forms, as, for example, the antecedent of 'If Bizet and Verdi had been compatriots then Bizet would have been Italian' and 'If Bizet and Verdi had been compatriots then Verdi would have been French'. There is thus no question of adjudicating between these statements: we are justified in affirming either.

49. May we not say that there is no question of adjudicating between them because *both are true*? We have, via the concept of a hypothetical variant, an analogical footing for predicating 'true' of a hypothetical, but since the clause forming a hypothetical is not a proposition, there is no question of giving the conditions under which such a statement is true.

50. For this same reason we are not able to express the principle of a *modus ponens* by a general hypothetical *corresponding* to the argument schema. Having resort again to the concept of a hypothetical variant, we arrive at the formulation: 'If Q is γ-inferable from $P_1, \ldots, P_n$ and if $P_1, \ldots, P_n$ are true then Q is true.' (Q is γ-inferable from $P_1, \ldots, P_n$ just in case there is some (possibly empty) set of *true* propositions from which, together with $P_1, \ldots, P_n$, Q is inferable.)

51. This may seem the height of paradox, because the major premiss of a

modus ponens, being a hypothetical, does not assert of some proposition that it is γ-inferable from others. But it only seems such if we overlook the distinction between argument form and root form.

52. The principles of *modus ponens* and *modus tollens* relate not to this or that form of logical inference, but to the logical form of inference as such. There is thus a certain irony in the fact that in the tradition they should be brought under the same hat as the principle of disjunctive syllogism.

53. Where the argument form of an argument is different from its root form, it needs to be shown that the alleged principle of the argument serves to explain how an argument with that argument form is valid. How the explanation runs in the case of a *modus ponens*.

54. In formulating the principle of an argument with a hypothetical conclusion as well as a hypothetical premiss, the notion of γ-inferability enters in connection with both conclusion and premiss. This is illustrated by formulating the principle of an incomplete *modus ponens*. How the formulated principle serves to explain the validity of such a form of argument.

55. Since the conjunction that generates a hypothetical is not a logical constant, it follows that there is no logic of the hypothetical *as such*. But it follows from the very facts that show this that any formally valid argument with hypothetical premisses and/or conclusion – saving only a degenerate argument – converts into a logically valid argument under replacement of the hypotheticals by the corresponding material conditionals.

56. Concluding remarks.

Text

1. Logic is the science or theory of argument that is valid in virtue of its form alone, irrespective of whatever matter may be contained in the premisses or conclusion. An argument that is formally valid will therefore be one whose form belongs to logic: the form under which it is valid will be a *logical* form. Accordingly, if there is any argument whose form belongs to logic, it should be one such as

> (i) If Yeats died before 1940 then he was outlived by Eliot
> Yeats did die before 1940
> Therefore he was outlived by Eliot

in which the consequent of a hypothetical statement is inferred from that statement together with its antecedent, or the related

> (ii) If Eliot died in 1938 then he was outlived by Yeats
> Eliot was not outlived by Yeats
> Therefore he did not die in 1938

in which the contradictory of the antecedent of a hypothetical statement is inferred from that statement together with the contradictory of the consequent. Indeed in the tradition these arguments with a hypothetical premiss are viewed as paradigms of formally valid argument alongside

> (iii) It is not the case that both Yeats and Eliot died before 1940
> Yeats died before 1940
> Therefore Eliot did not die before 1940

in which the major premiss is the denial of a conjunction, and

> (iv) Either Eliot or Yeats died before 1940
> Eliot did not die before 1940
> Therefore Yeats died before 1940

in which the major premiss is a disjunction. Together they are seen as forming a quartet exemplifying the four classical modes of inference known as *modus ponendo ponens*, *modus tollendo tollens*, *modus ponendo tollens* and *modus tollendo ponens*, and as the form under which (iii) is valid is represented by the schema

> Not both *p* and *q*
>
> *p*
>
Therefore not-*q*

and that under which (iv) is valid by the schema

> Either *p* or *q*
>
> Not-*p*
>
Therefore *q*

so the forms under which (i) and (ii) are valid are represented by the schemas

> If *p* then *q*
>
> *p*
>
Therefore *q*,

> If *p* then *q*
>
> Not-*q*
>
Therefore not-*p*

where the schematic letters stand in for propositions – expressions for truth-values.

2. We should therefore expect these latter forms, which involve the notion of a hypothesis, to belong to logic, along with the forms involving disjunction and conjunction. However, the difference between

(v)   Either Eliot or Yeats died before 1940
Therefore if Eliot did not die before 1940 then Yeats did

where the conclusion is a hypothetical – a statement of the same form as the major premiss of the *modus ponens* – and argument (iv), which contains no such statement, is not one of *logical* form: if I begin by presenting the disjunctive syllogism, but then become uncertain of the truth of the second premiss and so withdraw to the argument in which the proposition 'Eliot did not die before 1940' is introduced as a hypothesis instead of being asserted, I change not my logical, but my *dialectical*, stance. And indeed how, we might ask, should it not be possible to construct an argument with the *same* logical form as (iv), but one so articulated that it accommodates the speaker's doubt as to the truth of one of the premisses of the disjunctive syllogism? How could the concept of such an argument be incoherent?

Hence the step from (iv) to (v) is not on the same footing as that which I take if I withdraw (iv) in favour of

(vi)   Either Eliot or Yeats died before 1940
Therefore Eliot did not die before 1940 → Yeats died before 1940

where the conclusion is a truth-functional statement, asserting a material conditional. Here the transition is logical, with an argument of one logical form giving place to an argument of a *different* logical form, and it can be shown, of course, that if (iv) is valid then so is (vi). If we are inclined to assimilate the transition from (iv) to (v) to that from (iv) to (vi), that is because in either case I dispense with an argument having two premisses in favour of a single-premissed argument, and we assume that different arguments can only have the same logical form if they have the same number of premisses. But this assumption, however natural it may seem, is a prejudice. This becomes evident once we appreciate the mode of assertion that characterises a hypothetical and the consequent role of such statements in inference.

Now identity of logical form between (v) and (iv) means that the particle forming a hypothetical statement, unlike that forming a material conditional, is not a *logical* constant. For it is clear that there can be no argument of the form

Either p or q
Therefore not-p χ q

where 'χ' represents a logical constant, with the *same* logical form as (iv). We seem therefore forced to accept that the forms under which (i) and (ii) are valid are not logical forms, notwithstanding their absence of content.

So what, then, becomes of our understanding of logic as the theory of *formal* inference?

3. The difficulty is a real one and cannot be avoided by denying that (v) and (iv) do have the same logical form. There is perhaps no chapter in the history of logic which is so beset with difficulties as that involving inferences in which hypothetical statements figure, whether as premisses or conclusion or both, and a necessary first step towards their resolution is the recognition that if an argument α is related to an argument β as (v) is related to (iv) then α will have the same logical form as β – provided, of course, that β is valid under a logical form in the first place.

The recognition is almost immediate once it is acknowledged that the logical form of an argument is independent of whether its *limbs* – as we may call those propositions upon whose forms the validity of the argument depends – are *asserted*. We can no more fail to acknowledge this than we can fail to acknowledge that the logical form of an argument is independent of whether its limbs are *true*. It is granted that in giving the logical form of (iv) we have followed the common practice of logicians and represented it by a schema of the argument and this schema – since (iv) is a disjunctive syllogism – is the schema of an argument whose limbs are all asserted, but it is evident that we could also have given the logical form of (iv) by adverting to the *principle* of the argument, which finds expression in the *general* hypothetical 'If p or q and if not-p then q'. For the logical form of the argument is constituted by the formal relation that obtains between the first two limbs of the syllogism and the third through their being (corresponding) propositions of the forms p *or* q, *not-p*, q – a relation which we may symbolise by simply inserting a colon between the first two schemas and the third.

Now surely it goes without saying that two limbs of an argument may stand to a third limb in the relation p *or* q, *not-p* : q without being asserted.

4. Not so, it may be objected: two propositions may stand to a third in the given relation without being asserted, but not two limbs of an argument. We have to remember that not any piece of reasoning counts as an argument. An argument is at least a piece of reasoning in which an inference is drawn to an *assertion* and so typically concludes 'so . . .' or 'therefore . . .'. The conclusion may either follow on the heels of another assertion or assertions, as the examples of §1 illustrate, or what precedes the conclusion may itself be a piece of reasoning, as in an argument by *reductio ad absurdum*, where you begin by framing a supposition, from which you then infer propositions that contradict one another. But if you were to stop there, and not conclude with a denial of the proposition supposed to be true, thus discharging the supposition with which you began, you would have no argument; and by the same token

> Suppose that either Eliot or Yeats died before 1940
> Suppose, further, that Eliot did not die before 1940
Then Yeats died before 1940

is *so far* no argument, nothing having been asserted, although it is a piece of reasoning with the same logical form as (iv). So whilst we may concede that the logical form of a piece of reasoning is independent of how the propositions that constitute its limbs are presented, whether they be asserted or only supposed to be true, it remains true that if the piece of reasoning is an argument then it must contain those propositions as asserted. And from this it follows that an argument must be a disjunctive syllogism if it is to have the logical form of such.

In reply we may agree that an argument must conclude with an assertion, but the objection goes wrong to infer from this that the limbs of an argument must all be asserted, so that an argument will only have the logical form of a disjunctive syllogism if the forms *p or q*, *not-p* and *q* are exemplified by asserted propositions. It is true, of course, that an argument of this form in which the *q*-proposition is asserted will be one in which the disjunctive and negative propositions are asserted too – or, if not actually asserted, at least posited as true (*vide* §10) – but in drawing the above inference the objection assumes that the conclusion of an argument can only be a statement asserting a proposition, an expression for a truth-value, and what we are calling a hypothetical is not a statement of this kind. In making the disjunctive statement that either Eliot or Yeats died before 1940, I am indeed putting a proposition – a complex proposition – forward as true, but in asserting on this ground that if Eliot did not die before 1940 then Yeats did, I am doing no such thing. With a hypothetical statement it is the *mode of assertion* that is complex and not a propositional content.

It will be convenient to call a statement *simply assertoric* if it is one whose mode of assertion consists in putting a proposition forward as true.

5. As a statement that may serve as the major premiss of a *modus ponens*, a (singular) hypothetical is a statement in which one or more propositions (the antecedents) are introduced as hypotheses, with some further proposition (the consequent) being introduced as one whose truth is somehow consequent upon the truth of the antecedents. Thus we represent such a statement as having the form 'If p_1, ..., p_n then q', where it is understood, of course, that a statement of this form need not be in the indicative mood. 'If today were Tuesday then tomorrow would be Wednesday', no less than 'If today is Tuesday then tomorrow is Wednesday', is a hypothetical and introduces the truth of one proposition as somehow consequent upon the truth of another.

A general hypothetical, such as one expressing a principle of inference, will then be a hypothetical that is *exemplified by* one that is singular.

A proposition is an expression for a truth-value and so it is a matter of indifference whether we write the premiss of (i) in the words there given or by saying 'If it is true that Yeats died before 1940 then it is true that he was outlived by Eliot', where the propositional prefix is not to be taken as introducing an oblique clause: here the words 'it is true that Yeats died before 1940' and 'it is true that he was outlived by Eliot' are simply more explicit ways of forming the propositions already introduced by 'it is true that' and we might use 'it is the case that' to the same end. This means that if, for whatever reason, the expression following the prefix fails of a truth-value and so is not a genuine proposition, then the same is true of the expression with the prefix attached.

We remark in passing that what is here called a hypothetical statement, some logicians refer to as a *conditional* statement. The justification for the practice is that the subordinate clause of a hypothetical is known grammatically as a 'conditional clause'. It is to be observed, however, that the class of statements formed with a conditional clause is wider that the class of hypotheticals.

Now it follows from this representation of the form of a hypothetical that the subordinate clause(s) lie *outside* the scope of the main verb, otherwise the main clause of 'If Yeats died before 1940 then he was outlived by Eliot' would not constitute a proposition *of itself* and so could not be represented by a propositional letter. For it is clear that if the subordinate clause of a statement lies *within* the scope of the main verb and that verb is the main verb of a proposition then that proposition must embrace the subordinate clause. Thus in respect of the scope of the main verb, a hypothetical is on all fours with a statement formed with the ratiocinative 'since', such as 'Since Yeats died before 1940, he was outlived by Eliot', or with a concessive statement, such as 'Although Yeats was born in 1865, his greatest poems were written after 1920', in both of which, of course, the main clause is asserted.

From this simple grammatical consideration it can be seen that a hypothetical statement is not simply assertoric. For it is plainly a necessary, though not sufficient, condition of a statement's being such that any subordinate clause should lie within the scope of the main verb – as does, for instance, that of 'Yeats died before Eliot composed *Little Gidding*'. There is no form of statement '*q* before *p*' and this statement, despite its complexity, is one putting forward a certain temporal proposition as true, in which respect it is no different from the statement that Yeats died before 1940. If, however, this condition fails and a statement contains a subordinate clause that lies outside the scope of the main verb, it is evident that the form of that clause must itself bear upon the linguistic act effected by the statement's utterance, in which case it will be the mode of assertion that is complex and not a propositional content.

We reserve until later an account of the mode of assertion contained in a hypothetical – of how it contrasts with that contained in a statement that is simply assertoric.

6. Let us remember that it is only together with what the *Tractatus* calls its 'logico-syntactic employment' that a sign determines a logical form.[1] By no means every statement formed with 'if' is a hypothetical, and we distinguish, for example, between 'If Black is in need of another drink, there is some wine left in the decanter' and 'If Black is in need of another drink, he is in danger of becoming an alcoholic', recognising that in the former statement there is no question of introducing one proposition as a hypothesis and then introducing another as a proposition whose truth is somehow consequent upon it. Thus 'there is some wine left in the decanter' is here asserted, as comes out in the fact that the statement can be recast to read 'There is some wine left in the decanter, in case Black is in need of another drink'. Then

again, it would be absurd to argue 'If Black is in need of another drink, there is some wine left in the decanter: therefore if there is no wine left in the decanter, Black is not in need of another drink'. A hypothetical, on the other hand, can always be validly contraposed and it is is essentially all one whether we assert that if Black is in need of another drink, he is in danger of becoming an alcoholic or that if he is not in danger of becoming an alcoholic, he is not in need of another drink. A hypothetical and its contrapositive are, so to speak, sides of the same coin and either is immediately inferable from the other.[2]

Whilst this example is of a statement whose main clause is a proposition, albeit an asserted one, many statements formed with 'if' do not count as hypotheticals because the subordinate clause lies *within* the scope of the main verb. A clear example of such is a statement containing a conditional prediction. The syntactic employment of 'If the wind drops, it will rain' is no different from that of 'When the wind drops, it will rain' in so far as the main verb has wide scope in both. This agreement notwithstanding, it seems evident that the former statement does not assert a certain complex proposition, any more than does a hypothetical, where the subordinate clause lies outside the scope of the main verb. Indeed so much is implied by its description as a statement containing a *conditional* prediction.

To point up the difference between such a statement and a hypothetical, let us suppose that I know the disposition of the pieces in a game of chess up to White's last move, and so have reason to assert 'If White has moved his king's bishop to KB5 then Black is in a position to attack his queen'. This statement will then be understood as a hypothetical, expandable into 'If it is true that White has moved his king's bishop to KB5 then it is true that Black is in a position to attack his queen'. Let us suppose further that I am familiar with Black's abilities and habits of play and venture the prediction 'If White has moved his king's bishop to KB5, Black will attack his queen', or more idiomatically, 'Black will attack White's queen if he has moved his king's bishop to KB5'. It now stands out that this is no hypothetical if we compare it with the conclusion of the simple argument

> One of the propositions 'White has not moved his bishop to KB5', 'Black will attack White's queen' is true
> Therefore if (it is true that) White has moved his bishop to KB5, (it is true that) Black will attack White's queen

for it is palpable that the statement inferred here is no *prediction*, conditional or otherwise.

The statement containing the conditional prediction may assume the form 'If White has moved his bishop, I predict that Black will attack his queen', where the main clause now contains a verb with a performative role.[3] Then it is evident that the subordinate clause lies within the scope of the performative verb, for in uttering this sentence I am plainly not predicting that Black will attack White's queen, as I should be in uttering, say, 'Since White has moved his bishop, I predict that Black will attack his queen'. On the other hand, a hypothetical with the main clause 'I predict that Black will attack White's queen' would have to contain the *proposition* formed by those words. An example would be the conclusion of the argument

> I am familiar with Black's mode of play
> Therefore if everyone familiar with Black's mode of play predicts that he will attack White's queen then I predict that he will attack White's queen

where, to avoid misunderstanding, it would be natural to introduce the main clause of the hypothetical by 'it is true that' to show that, as the verb of a proposition, 'predict' does not here have its performative role.

The main verb has wide scope in any mode of discourse expressing a conditional speech act and in this respect we may compare the conditional prediction with the exhortation 'If White has moved his bishop, attack his queen' or, again, with the resolution 'I shall attack White's queen if he has moved his bishop'. In all such cases the *if*-clause is strictly adverbial to the main verb.

Failure to discern the character of a hypothetical as a statement in which the scope of the main verb is confined to the main clause may lead one to reject as invalid forms of argument that are patently valid. One such form of argument is that exemplified by a hypothetical syllogism. Suppose, for example, that being privy to Black's strategy, I have reason to assert that if White has moved his king's bishop to KB5, Black will attack his queen and yet do *not* have reason to assert – this being no part of Black's strategy – that if White has moved his king's bishop (moved it as such), Black will attack his queen. Suppose, however, that at the same time I have grounds, unknown perhaps to Black, for making the hypothetical assertion that if White has moved his king's bishop then he has moved it to KB5. Does this then cast doubt on the validity of the form of argument *If p then q; if q then r: therefore if p then r*? Not at all! But if I do not distinguish hypotheticals from *if*-statements in which the subordinate clause lies within the scope of the main verb, I may be led to conclude that it does.[4]

7. Thus von Wright is guilty of grammatical confusion when he writes:

> I shall never speak of the conditional as a proposition which is being asserted, but only of propositions being asserted, relative to other pro-positions. Therefore we must not say that 'if p, then q', when used to assert q on the condition p, expresses something which is either true or false. But we shall certainly have to agree to saying that a proposition

may be truly or falsely asserted conditionally, relative to another proposition.[5]

The idea is that in making a statement of the form *If p then q*, I am not asserting a (complex) proposition because the act of making such a statement is a conditional one: the assertion I am making is conditional in the sense in which we speak of a conditional bet or conditional command. So on this view the hypothetical 'If today is Tuesday then tomorrow is Wednesday' could take the form 'If today is Tuesday then I assert that tomorrow is Wednesday', with a performative verb in the main clause, as in the case of the conditional prediction. But, as we have seen, this is not possible. A hypothetical with this wording would not introduce the proposition 'this is Tuesday', but the proposition 'I assert that tomorrow is Wednesday', as one whose truth is somehow consequent upon that of 'today is Tuesday'!

Let us not be misled here by the word 'condition'. A hypothetical can indeed be characterised as a statement in which one proposition is asserted on the condition of the truth of another (others), but this is not to say that the act of uttering such a statement is a conditional one. As we shall see in §27, a statement in which one proposition is asserted on the condition of the truth of another is to be compared with a statement in which one proposition is asserted on the ground of the truth of another – a statement which is likewise not simply assertoric. As we distinguish between a statement asserting one proposition *on the ground* of the truth of another and one asserting that the truth of one proposition *is* a ground for the truth of another, which is simply assertoric, so we distinguish between a statement asserting one proposition *on the condition* of the truth of another and one asserting that the truth of one proposition *is* a (sufficient) condition of the truth of another.

8. As we have indicated, the hypothetical form of statement does not only comprehend statements that are grammatically indicative. In both

> If Keynes is married to a Russian ballerina then some Cambridge economist is married to a Russian ballerina
> Keynes is married to a Russian ballerina
> Therefore some Cambridge economist is married to a Russian ballerina,

> If Keynes were married to a Russian ballerina then some Cambridge economist would be married to a Russian ballerina
> But Keynes is married to a Russian ballerina
> Therefore some Cambridge economist is married to a Russian ballerina

we have an argument by *modus ponens*, despite the difference in mood of the two major premisses. Using our prefix, we could write these as 'If it is (were) true that Keynes is married to a Russian ballerina then it is (would be) true that some Cambridge economist is married to a Russian ballerina', to emphasise their common identity as hypotheticals incorporating the same propositions as antecedent and consequent. These propositions do not appear on the surface of the major premiss of the second *modus ponens*, but we say that its author is uttering a hypothetical with these propositions as antecedent and consequent *in that* it can be so written.

It is sometimes thought that use of the subjunctive form expresses the speaker's belief in the falsity of the antecedent, but if this were the case then someone who executed the above *modus ponens*, using the second wording, would be contradicting himself! Or, to make the same point in another way, you do not express the same belief twice if you say 'If Keynes were married to a Swedish ballerina, which he is not, then some Cambridge economist would be married to a Swedish ballerina'. No, the significance of the wording with 'were' and 'would' is not that it expresses the speaker's belief in the falsity of the antecedent but that it *allows for the concomitant expression of that belief* – and that it allows too, we should add, for the concomitant expression of his belief in the truth of the consequent. So, for example, a doctor might say of a patient 'If the virus from which he is suffering were an influenza virus then his throat would be inflamed, which, as we see, it is'. Not, of course, that the corresponding hypotheticals in the indicative do not allow for the concomitant expression of such beliefs, but this is not signified by their mood.

9. We argued in §3 that the logical form of an argument is independent of whether its limbs are all asserted and contended that if an argument α is related to an argument β as (v) is related to (iv) then α has the same logical form as β, notwithstanding that (v) has only one premiss while (iv) has two. If we thought, however, that two arguments could only have the same logical form if they had the same number of premisses, then we should be driven to conclude, contrary to §2, that the concept of an *argument* with the logical form of a disjunctive syllogism in which the disjunctive or negative limb was not asserted was, after all, incoherent.

For, as we now observe, the premisses of an argument cannot be modally mixed, with at least one being an assertion and at least one a supposition. We may draw an inference from mixed premisses, as in the hybrid formation

> Keynes is a Cambridge economist
> Suppose now he is married to a Russian ballerina
> Then some Cambridge economist is married to a Russian ballerina

but so far we have no argument, properly speaking, since the inferred proposition is not asserted. It is obvious that premisses that are modally mixed cannot yield as conclusion a proposition that is asserted. We have essentially the same inference (but again no argument) in

> Suppose that Keynes is married to a Russian ballerina: then, since he is a Cambridge economist, some Cambridge economist is married to a Russian ballerina

where the supposition occurs first and the proposition 'Keynes is a Cambridge economist', instead of being asserted outright, is now introduced by the conjunction 'since'. The syntactic pattern of this formation is therefore 'Suppose that *q*: then (since *p*), *r*' – not 'Suppose that *q*: then (since *p*, *r*)'! – with the *since*-clause lying outside the scope of the inferential particle. Thus whilst the form of words is the same, it does not contain the *statement* that occurs as the conclusion of

> Keynes is married to a Russian ballerina
> Therefore since he is a Cambridge economist, some Cambridge economist is married to a Russian ballerina

where the syntactic pattern is '*q*: therefore (since *p*, *r*)'. It helps to see this if we remember that alongside the hybrid formation we also have

> Suppose that Keynes were married to a Russian ballerina: then, since he is a Cambridge economist, some Cambridge economist would be married to a Russian ballerina

in which it stands out that the form of words following 'then' does not constitute a statement.

Given, then, that no argument is possible with an assertion and supposition as premisses, it follows that an argument having the same logical form as the syllogism relating to Keynes, but in which only the first or limb is asserted can have only one premiss. Assuming, then, that it is the first limb that is asserted, the argument will start from the single premiss that Keynes is a Cambridge economist, in which case the conclusion will be a statement containing 'Keynes is married to a Russian ballerina' and 'some Cambridge economist is married to a Russian ballerina' as component clauses, where the conjunction forming the statement introduces the first of these as a clause whose truth-value is left open, *in the way* the locution 'suppose that' leaves open the truth-value of the clause which it introduces. But the hypothetical is precisely such a statement, and the argument for which we are looking is

> Keynes is a Cambridge economist
> Therefore if Keynes is married to a Russian ballerina then some Cambridge economist is married to a Russian ballerina

in which the proposition that forms the second premiss of the syllogism is displaced to become the antecedent of a hypothetical. What shows that this argument has the same logical form, exemplifies the same principle, as the syllogism is the fact that we cannot discriminate in *logical* form between the reasoning here and the reasoning in what we have called above the hybrid formation. For different though the two reasonings are, the ground of their difference is simply that in the hybrid formation the proposition 'Keynes is married to a Russian ballerina' is introduced as a hypothesis through occurring as a clause in a sentence of the form 'Suppose that *p*', whereas in the argument it is so introduced through occurring as the antecedent of a hypothetical. Thus language, by providing the resources with which to form a hypothetical *statement*, makes it possible to convert a formation in which *R* is inferred from (an asserted proposition) *P together with* a hypothesis *Q* into an argument in which *R* is inferred from *P on the hypothesis of* (the truth of) *Q*.

The identity in logical form between the argument with the hypothetical conclusion and the corresponding syllogism comes out in various ways. So, for instance, to mark the fact that an argument is one whose principle belongs to logic, we may incorporate the expression 'of logical necessity' into the argument, in which case the syllogism will conclude

> Therefore of logical necessity some Cambridge economist is married to a Russian ballerina.

If we now incorporate this expression into the argument with the hypothetical conclusion, we may introduce it *before the consequent of the hypothetical*, so that the conclusion reads

> Therefore if Keynes is married to a Russian ballerina then of logical necessity some Cambridge economist is married to a Russian ballerina.

One lesson, then, of the present enquiry is that it is a mistake to assume that the inference contained in an argument has, so to speak, to keep in step with its principle, so that an argument can only exemplify a given principle if it contains as many premisses as the hypothetical expressing the principle contains *if*-clauses. An argument does not have to be a disjunctive syllogism in order to exemplify the principle *If p or q and if not-p then q*, and the argument above, no less than the corresponding argument with two premisses, exemplifies the principle *If Fa and if Ga then something (that is) F is G*.

In §2 we asked the rhetorical question, 'How should it not be possible to construct an argument with the same logical form as a disjunctive syllogism, but one so articulated that it accommodates the speaker's doubt as to the truth of one of the premisses?' Here we have sought to explain that it is through the concept of a hypothetical statement that such a construction is possible and with this explanation we have completed the proof that if an argument α is related to an argument β as (v) is related to (iv) then α has the same logical form as β.

10. It is not only through the concept of such a statement, however, that arguments are possible that have the same logical form, despite a difference in the number of their premisses. A conjunction with a grammar cognate to the 'if' of a hypothetical is 'since' in its ratiocinative employment, and statements formed by its means enjoy a similar role in argument. Thus in the single-premissed argument

(vii)   Either Eliot or Yeats died before 1940
Therefore since Eliot did not die before 1940, Yeats did

where the conclusion is what we shall call a *thetical* statement, we also have an argument with the same logical form as the disjunctive syllogism. It seems natural to call the conclusion here a thetical statement, because the antecedent is introduced as a *thesis*, as a proposition the speaker is *positing* the truth of rather than asserting outright.

It might be said, of course, that this same proposition – 'Eliot did not die before 1940' – is also introduced as a thesis in (iv), but there is a vital difference between its occurrence there and its occurrence in (vii). For in the disjunctive syllogism it is introduced as a thesis not because it is introduced by a certain conjunction, but because it forms a statement that is simply assertoric. Speaking strictly, the notion of a proposition's being introduced as a thesis is a *weaker* one than that of its being asserted: you cannot assert a proposition without positing it as true, but you can posit a proposition as true without asserting it – without uttering the corresponding assertoric sentence or (in certain cases) main clause of a sentence. An example of such is, of course, the main clause of a thetical itself.

It is worth remarking that there is an analogous distinction between introducing a proposition as a hypothesis, as when it is the antecedent of a hypothetical statement, and actually *framing it as a hypothesis*, as when it is prefaced by 'suppose that'. Here again the second notion is weaker than the first, for you cannot frame a proposition as a hypothesis without introducing it as a hypothesis, but you can do the latter without framing it as a hypothesis – without uttering a sentence running 'Suppose that *p*'.

Whilst there may be some who would question the identity of logical form between (v) and (iv), being wrongly persuaded, perhaps, that a hypothetical statement can be assimilated to a material conditional, it is hard to imagine that anyone would question the identity of logical form between (vii) and (iv). For without the acknowledgement of this identity, we should be at a loss to understand why – *what would otherwise confront us as an insurmountable paradox* – the validity of (vii) is not impugned by the fact that in drawing the thetical conclusion you commit yourself to the truth of both its antecedent and its consequent, neither of which is entailed by the premiss of the argument!

Thetical statements come into their own in forms of argument that presuppose the validity of other arguments and the truth of their premisses. Thus I accept as valid the argument

> (v) has the same logical form as (iv)
> Therefore the conjunction generating a hypothetical is not a logical constant

along with the argument

> The conjunction generating a hypothetical is not a logical constant
> Therefore an argument by *modus ponens* does not belong to propositional logic

and I recognise therewith that I am justified in arguing

> (v) has the same logical form as (iv)
> Therefore an argument by *modus ponens* does not belong to propositional logic

but how shall I express this recognition itself in the form of an argument? The answer is provided by an argument in which the premisses and conclusion are thetical statements corresponding to the three arguments above. We then have an argument running

> Since (v) has the same logical form of (iv), the conjunction generating a hypothetical is not a logical constant
> Since the conjunction generating a hypothetical is not a logical constant, an argument by *modus ponens* does not belong to propositional logic
> Therefore since (v) has the same logical form as (iv), an argument by *modus ponens* does not belong to propositional logic.

11. With the recognition that (v) and (vii) have the same logical form as (iv), we are brought to acknowledge the concept of a *dialectical variant* of an argument. In such a variant one or more premisses of the parent argument are dropped and the propositions asserted therein introduced as hypotheses or theses. In the former case we have a *hypothetical variant* of the parent argument and in the latter a *thetical variant*. It will become clear, as our investigation progresses, how vital the concept of a hypothetical variant is to an understanding of arguments in which hypothetical statements figure. This

is obviously true of arguments in which the conclusion is a hypothetical, but it is no less true of arguments with a hypothetical premiss or premisses. In particular, it is only through the concept of a hypothetical variant that we can vindicate the claim logic makes to be the science of formal inference when the form represented by the argument schema of a *modus ponens* is not a logical form.

Argument (v), then, is the hypothetical variant we obtain if we drop the second premiss of the disjunctive syllogism and introduce the negative proposition as a hypothesis. If instead we drop the first premiss of (iv) and introduce the disjunctive proposition as a hypothesis, we obtain the argument

> (viii)   Eliot did not die before 1940
> Therefore if Eliot or Yeats died before 1940 then Yeats died before 1940

as a hypothetical variant. Indeed since someone may begin by presenting (iv) and then become unsure of both the disjunctive and negative premiss, so that he wishes to drop both, we should admit the degenerate hypothetical variant

> (ix)   Therefore if Eliot or Yeats died before 1940 and if Eliot did not die before that date then Yeats died before 1940

in which a conclusion is drawn from 'the empty set of premisses'. It is true that our language does not provide for the formation of arguments with a conclusion and no premisses, but where the conclusion is a hypothetical, so that we can cite a normal argument with the same form, the concept of such an argument is perfectly intelligible.

Since (ix) has the same logical form as (iv), the inferred hypothetical exemplifies the principle of disjunctive syllogism and is thus put forward as one in which the consequent is inferable from the antecedents alone. Normally, of course, a person who uttered this complex hypothetical would be putting it forward as such anyway, since it is obvious that the consequent is inferable from the antecedents by themselves, but to introduce it as a conclusion from the empty set of premisses would be a way of *showing* that it was being put forward in this way.

12. Let us now call an argument whose premisses and conclusion are simply assertoric – an argument, that is, in which a proposition is asserted on the ground of the truth of other asserted propositions – a *standard* argument. Then since there are 2^n possibilities of assertion and non-assertion on the part of n propositions, a standard argument with n premisses will have $2^n - 1$ hypothetical variants if we admit the degenerate case. And given the same condition, it will, of course, have that number of thetical variants.

The classical definition of a valid argument – that an argument is valid if and only if it is impossible for (the propositions that form) the premises to be true without (the proposition that forms) the conclusion being true – is framed only for standard arguments. This does not mean, however, that it needs supplementing to provide for arguments with a hypothetical or thetical conclusion, like (v) and (vii). As dialectical variants, their validity simply reduces to the validity of the arguments of which they are variants.

Do the premises of a dialectical variant of a valid argument *entail* the conclusion? Or is the relation of entailment one that holds only between the premises and conclusion of a standard argument? It may be remembered that Moore proposed to use the term 'entails' as the converse of 'follows from', in the sense in which the conclusion of a syllogism in *Barbara* follows from its premises.[6] Now to say that the conclusion of a syllogism in *Barbara* follows from its premises is to say no more than that such an argument is a valid deductive argument, so *in this sense* of 'entails' the premiss of a (hypo) thetical variant of a syllogism may be described as entailing its conclusion, despite the fact that the conclusion is not a statement asserting a proposition. Only we have then to bear in mind that with this understanding of the term we cannot equate 'The premisses of the argument . . . entail the conclusion' with 'It is (logically) impossible for the premisses of . . . to be true without the conclusion being true'.

It is common practice, however, to ignore the provenance of the term and accept the semantic equation. This is the practice we have followed here, and with this understanding of 'entails' we shall not describe the premiss of a dialectical variant of an argument as entailing the conclusion. Of course, we shall not deny it either, as we have, for instance, denied in §10 that the premiss of (vii) entails the antecedent or consequent of the thetical conclusion. In the semantic understanding of the term, the statement that the premiss of (v) and (vii) does not entail the conclusion of these arguments can only be understood grammatically – as we understand the statement that a dandelion does not have teeth.

It is a great confusion to think that we can approach the question of the validity of a dialectical variant, as we can that of a standard argument, by asking whether it is possible that the premiss or premises should be true without the conclusion being true. That is simply to ignore their status as dialectical variants, as if (v) and (vii) acknowledged no parent but stood on their own with a logical form distinct from that of the disjunctive syllogism. Indeed the whole management of issues relating to the validity of this or that form of argument involving hypotheticals, whether these occur as premises or conclusion or both, has been bedevilled by the assumption that they are to be conducted in terms of the truth and falsity of such statements. This assumption cannot be sustained once it is realised that the simplest of such arguments – arguments in which a hypothetical conclusion is inferred from premises that are simply assertoric – are dialectical variants of arguments whose premises and conclusion alike are simply assertoric.

13. The statement that an argument has $2^n - 1$ hypothetical variants implies that we are counting

> Not-E
> Therefore if it were true that either E or Y then it would be true that Y

and (viii) as the same hypothetical variant under different forms. And likewise, of course

> Therefore if it were true that either E or Y and if it were true that not-E
> then it would be true that Y

and (ix). For the conclusion of these two variants allows for the concomitant expression of the speaker's belief in the falsity of the antecedent(s), or the truth of the consequent. It is only this that is signified by using the form with 'were' and 'would', whereas the indicative form leaves it open (*vide* §8). No such alternative form is possible for (v), however, and the reason is not far to seek. For it is evident that you may know a disjunction to be true, and know also that one of the disjuncts is false, without thereby having a ground for asserting the other disjunct. If your knowledge is to afford you with such a ground, so that you are in a position to argue as in (iv), you must believe the disjunction independently of believing either disjunct. Since therefore (v) enjoys the same principle of inference as (iv), it follows that the truth of the disjunction only affords you with a ground for asserting the hypothetical if your belief in it is likewise 'non-truth-functional', and this is why it cannot assume a form which allows for the concomitant expression of a belief in the falsity of the antecedent or the truth of the consequent.

14. The epistemic consideration that a truth-functional statement can only provide you with a ground for asserting a hypothetical if you believe it independently of believing the propositions expressing its truth-grounds,[7] explains why the use of the hypothetical form in a statement such as 'If Bacon wrote the plays of Shakespeare then pigs can fly', where the consequent is obviously false, counts as idiomatic. For it is apparent that the only ground the speaker could have for making this hypothetical statement is that it is not true both that Bacon wrote the plays of Shakespeare and that pigs cannot fly, but this is precisely not available to him because his belief in the truth-functional proposition derives from his belief that Bacon was not the author of the plays attributed to Shakespeare. The poet himself provides a nice example of the same idiom in the exchange between Macbeth and his wife when she scolds him for his unruly behaviour at the sight of Banquo's ghost (Act III, Scene IV). 'When all's done', she says, 'You look but on a stool', and he responds with 'If I stand here, I saw him'. Here it is evident that Macbeth's ground for his assertion can only consist in the truth of the

proposition that denies the conjunction of the antecedent of his hypothetical with the negation of its consequent. But he does not believe this truth-functional proposition independently of believing that he saw Banquo. Hence the idiom.

It should be obvious that it is wrong to cite such cases as evidence that the particle 'if' sometimes has the sense of '→'. If Macbeth's statement were really a material conditional, and thus logically equivalent to 'It is not the case both that I stand here and that I did not see him' – in which case, let us remember, the word 'if' therein would not have the grammar of a subordinating conjunction – where on earth would be the *idiom*?

15. It is this same consideration which undermines the defence that Quine, in blithe disregard of grammar, seeks to make for the analysis of hypothetical statements – at least those in the indicative mood – as material conditionals. Quine remarks that we find such statements as

> If France is in Europe then the sea is salt
> If France is in Australia then the sea is salt
> If France is in Australia then the sea is sweet

strange because 'it is not usual in practice' to form hypotheticals out of propositions whose truth or falsity is already known. For, he asks, why affirm either of the first two statements when we are in a position to affirm the stronger statement that the sea is salt? And why affirm the third when we are in a position to affirm the stronger statement that France is not in Australia?[8] Now certainly we find such statements strange, but this is not for the reason that Quine thinks. It is not a question here of not making a weaker statement when we are in a position to make a stronger. Let us grant that as a rule we do not, at least without further ado, make a weaker statement when we are in a position to make a stronger, so that we should not normally assert the material conditionals corresponding to the above hypotheticals. Still, this is not the *explanation* why we are not disposed to affirm the statements in Quine's list. The explanation is that the only thing we know which could serve as a ground for affirming them is the truth of the corresponding truth-functional proposition and this, as we have seen, is not available to us as such a ground because we do not believe it independently of believing the propositions which express its truth-grounds. If, however, we may suppose one of Quine's readers to be ignorant of the truth-values of the antecedent and consequent of these same hypotheticals and to know the corresponding truth-functional proposition on grounds of testimony, then he would not share our attitude towards them. To him they would not appear strange.

If we found such hypotheticals strange for the reason Quine gives then we should not be disposed to assert either of

If France is in Australia then France is both not in Australia and in
Australia
If (the sea is salt → the sea is salt) then the sea is salt

for we are in no doubt about the truth-values of the antecedent and consequent of these two statements! But, of course, we have no hesitation in
asserting either hypothetical, our ground in the first case being that France is
not in Australia and in the second that the sea is salt. These examples thus
demonstrate that it is wrong to think that you can never ground a hypothetical assertion on the falsity of its antecedent or the truth of its consequent. Only we observe that where this is the case, this is not *because* the
proposition expressing the ground contradicts the antecedent or coincides
with the consequent. Thus the form under which the first of these hypotheticals is assertible on the ground of the falsity of its antecedent is the same as
the form under which the argument

France is a founder member of the European Community
Therefore if France has a large rural population then France is both a
founder member of the European Community and has a large
rural population

is valid, and the form under which the second one is assertible on the ground
of the truth of its consequent is the same as the form under which the
argument

Deposits of sodium chloride were formed when the earth
cooled
Therefore if (deposits of sodium chloride were formed when the earth
cooled → the sea is salt) then the sea is salt

is valid. Here the first of these arguments is a hypothetical variant of an
argument whose principle is *If p and if q then both p and q* and the second
is a hypothetical variant of an argument whose principle is *If p and if p → q*
then q.

16. As logicians we are inclined to take for granted the notion of the form
under which an argument is valid, and we have ourselves made use of it in
these investigations. Indeed this whole enquiry began with the difficulty of
understanding how logic can make good its claim to be the science of formal
inference, when it appears that the form under which an argument by *modus
ponens* or *modus tollens* is valid is not a logical form. For arguments such as
(i) and (ii) are amongst our paradigms of what constitutes a formally valid
argument. Our discussion has disclosed, however, that this uncritical acceptance of the notion of *the* form under which an argument is valid is a mistake.

For once we have the concept of a dialectical variant of an argument, it is borne upon us that what are called different forms of argument – arguments as different in form as the disjunctive syllogism and its various hypothetical and thetical variants – can all share the same logical form, and with this realisation it becomes evident that we operate in our thinking with two distinct notions of the form of an argument. Accordingly, there are two ways of construing the expression 'the form under which the argument . . . is valid'. Understood dialectically, it alludes to what we shall call the *argument form* of an argument, which is different in an argument and its dialectical variants. Understood as that which is common to an argument and its variants, it alludes to what we shall call the *root form* of an argument.

Logical form is then a special case of root form.

17. The argument form of an argument is the form under which it is valid *as an inference from such and such premisses to such and such a conclusion.* Accordingly, arguments that differ in the number of their premisses will differ in their argument forms. In many cases, the argument form of an argument will be represented by what logicians call an argument schema, and indeed it can always be so represented if the argument is a standard one. Thus the argument form of (iv) is represented by the schema

> Either p or q
> Not-p
Therefore q

which we deployed in §1 to represent its logical form. The three sub-schemas 'q', 'either p or q', 'not-p' represent the respective forms under which the conclusion of the disjunctive syllogism is inferable from the two premisses. Again, the argument form of (i), although not a standard argument, is represented by the schema

> If p then q
> p
Therefore q

in which, again, the three sub-schemas represent the forms under which the conclusion of the *modus ponens* is inferable from its premisses. As we have seen, however, in this case the schema does not represent a logical form, despite its purely formal character. The argument form of (v), on the other hand, cannot be represented by a schema of the argument. It may seem strange to say this, for anyone who presents an argument of the form

> Either p or q
Therefore if not-p then q

inferring a hypothetical conclusion from a disjunctive premiss, is framing a hypothetical variant of a disjunctive syllogism and *thereby* presenting a valid argument. (It is understood, of course, that the hypothetical, being inferred from such a premiss, has here the indicative form.) The point is, however – and the point is one that is vital for an understanding of the role of hypotheticals in argument –that an argument *of* this form is not valid *under* this form. That is to say, the conclusion of (v) is not inferable from its premiss in that they have the respective forms *if not-p then q, either p or q.* The hypothetical variant thus stands in marked contrast to the argument with a disjunctive premiss and a material conditional as conclusion. For here the conclusion *is*, of course, inferable from the premiss in that they have the respective forms *not-p → q, either p or q.*

Speaking generally, the argument form of a dialectical variant – at least one that is not degenerate – cannot be represented by a schema of the argument.

18. To see that (v) is not valid under the form represented by the displayed schema, let us take in place of (v) the hypothetical variant

> Either the water in the glass is hot or cold
> Therefore if it is not hot then it is cold

but now let us suppose, since we all sometimes speak without thinking, that someone should assert 'If the water in the glass is not hot then it is cold', intending this statement as one would normally intend, say, 'If the sky is not overcast then it is free from cloud'. That is to say, his statement is to be read as if it were the conclusion of the (degenerate) hypothetical variant of the argument in which 'The water in the glass is cold' is (invalidly) inferred from 'The water in the glass is not hot'. So he is in effect excluding the possibility of the water's being neither hot nor cold. It is obvious, however, that the hypothetical inferred in the above variant of the disjunctive syllogism does not admit of this strong reading.

Or suppose again that someone should fail to see that 'Russell admires someone who admires himself' is deducible from the single premiss 'Russell admires himself' and should argue

> It is not the case both that Russell admires himself and does not admire someone who admires himself
> Therefore if Russell admires himself then he admires someone who admires himself

simply taking on trust the truth-functional premiss. We shall then read his hypothetical differently from the hypothetical which serves as the conclusion of the (degenerate) hypothetical variant of the argument whose principle is *If a has R to itself then a has R to something that has R to itself* – the single-premissed argument in which 'Russell admires someone who admires himself' is deduced from 'Russell admires himself'. On the weak reading, the hypothetical will not exemplify the reflexive principle and the author of the statement will not be excluding the possibility of Russell's admiring himself but not admiring someone who admires himself.

There is therefore a sense in which the description of a statement as a hypothetical with such and such antecedents and consequent does not fully determine that statement. To say this is not to deny that the hypothetical form of statement is *one* form, but, as these examples show, that form is *dialectically ambiguous*. A statement of this form is, so to speak, in thrall to the hypothetical variant of which it is to be seen as the conclusion. This does not mean, of course, that such a variant needs to have been formulated by a speaker or to be present in his mind when giving utterance to a hypothetical.

19. How, then, are we to convey the argument form of a hypothetical variant of an argument when that form cannot be represented by an argument schema? The terms of the question itself suggest the answer. Since representation of the argument form by a schema is impossible, we have to resort to a description and this description must allude to the fact of the hypothetical variant's *being a variant of such and such a form of argument*. Thus a description of the argument form of (v) will allude to its being a hypothetical variant of a disjunctive syllogism and so will run:

> *the form which (v) has as a hypothetical variant of a disjunctive syllogism in which the second or minor premiss is dropped.*

And now the thought may occur to us that *if* we could represent the argument form of (v) by a schema of the argument as we can that of (vi) – the corresponding argument with a material conditional as conclusion – and so convey it *without* having resort to a description that alludes to the form of the argument of which it is a hypothetical variant, then we could no more identify the logical form of (v) with that of the disjunctive syllogism than we can identify the logical form of (vi) with that of the disjunctive syllogism! We distinguish the argument form of a hypothetical variant from its logical form, but we cannot identify the former without importing the notion of the latter.

The reader may easily assure himself that a thetical statement is subject to this same dialectical ambiguity, so that the argument form of a thetical variant too can only be conveyed by alluding to the form of the argument of which it is a variant. Thus the argument form of (vii) is the form it has as a thetical variant of a disjunctive syllogism in which the minor premiss is dropped.

20. If the argument form of a hypothetical variant cannot be represented by an argument schema then neither, of course, can that of an argument in which a hypothetical is inferred from a hypothetical premiss or premisses. Thus it will be a consequence of the dialectical ambiguity of the hypothetical form of statement that the argument form of an argument by contraposition, for example, or a hypothetical syllogism cannot be represented by a schema of the argument.

Let us begin, first, with argument by contraposition. It is plain that an argument of the form

> If p then q
> Therefore if not-q then not-p

being one in which a given hypothetical is contraposed, is a valid argument, but the schema does not represent the form under which the contrapositive of a hypothetical is inferable from that hypothetical. To be sure, if you draw the inference

> If Russell admires himself then he admires someone who admires himself
> Therefore if he does not admire someone who admires himself then he does not admire himself

the second hypothetical will be the contrapositive of the first – it will be such because it is inferred from it – but the point to remark is that one hypothetical is not the contrapositive of another *merely* in virtue of bearing to it the formal relation *if not-q then not-p : if p then q*. We cannot model the contraposition of a hypothetical statement upon that of a material conditional.

This means that to convey the argument form of the above argument – the form under which it is valid as an inference from 'If Russell admires himself then he admires someone who admires himself' to 'If Russell does not admire someone who admires himself then he does not admire himself' – we have once more to resort to a description. This description, as with a hypothetical variant of an argument, must allude to the concept of such a variant, only in the present case, where both premiss and conclusion are hypotheticals, the concept of a hypothetical variant makes a double entrance. Thus if we employ the expression 'variant relevant to the hypothetical *h*' as short for 'the variant of which the hypothetical *h* is to be seen as the conclusion', the argument form of the above argument will be conveyed by deploying its argument schema and adding the description: *in which the parent of the variant relevant to the conclusion is the result of contraposing the parent of the variant relevant to the premiss.* So if the premiss of this argument has the truth-functional ground then the parent of the variant relevant to the conclusion will be

> It is not the case both that Russell admires himself and does not admire someone who admires himself
> Russell does not admire someone who admires himself
> Therefore he does not admire himself

because this argument is the result of contraposing

> It is not the case both that Russell admires himself and does not admire someone who admires himself
> Russell admires himself
> Therefore he admires someone who admires himself

whereas if the premiss exemplifies the reflexive principle, the parent of the variant relevant to the conclusion will be

> Russell does not admire someone who admires himself
> Therefore he does not admire himself.

Similar considerations apply to an argument in which a hypothetical conclusion is inferred from a hypothetical premiss or premisses, as, for example, the hypothetical syllogism

> If Moore admires himself then he admires Russell
> If Moore admires Russell then he admires someone who admires himself
> Therefore if Moore admires himself then he admires someone who admires himself

where it is, of course, clear that the conclusion does *not* exemplify the reflexive principle! So for this very reason we recognise that the argument form of this argument cannot be represented by the schema

> If p then q
> If q then r
> Therefore if p then r.

An argument of this form is indeed valid, but to convey its argument form we need a description which specifies that the parent of the variant relevant to the conclusion is the 'transitive heir' of the parents of the variants that are relevant to the two premisses. This means that if the parent of the variant relevant to the first premiss is the argument

It is not the case both that Moore admires himself and that he
does not admire Russell
Moore admires himself
Therefore Moore admires Russell

and the parent of the variant relevant to the second premiss is the argument

Russell admires himself
Moore admires Russell
Therefore Moore admires someone who admires himself

then the parent of the variant relevant to the conclusion will be the argument

It is not the case both that Moore admires himself and that he
does not admire Russell
Moore admires himself
Russell admires himself
Therefore Moore admires someone who admires himself.

21. With our conception of a hypothetical variant, it is clear that we are not
able to agree with Frege when he speaks in his *Begriffsschrift* of the causal
connection that is contained in the word 'if', and argues that if we render the
'if' of 'If the Moon is (now) in quadrature with the Sun, then she appears
semi-circular' with the conditional stroke – the sign which in his ideography
serves to express a material conditional – this connection will not be
expressed.[9] For if it were part of the meaning of the conjunction 'if' to import
such a connection, how could the argument

It is not the case both that the Moon is (now) in quadrature
with the Sun and that she does not appear semi-circular
The Moon is (now) in quadrature with the Sun
Therefore she appears semi-circular

have as a hypothetical variant an argument with the conclusion 'If the Moon
is (now) in quadrature with the Sun, then she appears semi-circular'? Of
course, we read Frege's hypothetical differently from that which is asserted on
the truth-functional ground, identifying it rather with that which forms the
conclusion of the (degenerate) hypothetical variant of the physical argument

The Moon is (now) in quadrature with the Sun
So she appears semi-circular

and this perhaps explains why he should speak of the 'if' in his example as
containing a causal connection. For he goes on to say in the same passage
that 'this connection is something general' and this is true in the sense that the

conclusion of the hypothetical variant of the physical argument exemplifies the principle of that argument – a principle which finds its natural expression in the form of a general hypothetical. We may take it to run something like 'If a (spherical) heavenly body is in quadrature with the Sun at time t then it presents a semi-circular appearance at time t'.

22. How crucial the concept of a hypothetical variant is to the understanding of inferences in which hypotheticals figure! In particular, the difficulties encountered by logicians in understanding the relationship of hypothetical statements to truth-functional ones, with some even going so far as to deny that a hypothetical can be validly inferred from a truth-functional statement, have their resolution in the concept of a hypothetical variant.

The epitome of these difficulties confronts us at the very beginning of our logical studies. For as soon as we are introduced to propositional logic, we are naturally exercised by the nature of hypothetical statements and their relation to truth-functional ones, and then we cannot help being puzzled by the fact that arguments such as the following

$$A \to B$$
$$A$$
Therefore B,

Not both A and not-B
Therefore A $\to$ B

whose forms belong to propositional logic, seem undeniably to have valid counterparts in the corresponding arguments with a hypothetical as premiss and conclusion in place of the material conditional. (Here the capital letters are to be thought of as actual propositions.) For we are baffled to understand how the counterpart arguments could be valid unless the hypothetical were itself a truth-functional statement, with the same truth-conditions as the material conditional.[10] In which case we should be no less justified in reading 'A $\to$ B' in the above inferences as 'If A then B' than we are, say, in reading the premiss and conclusion of

$$A \lor B$$
$$\text{Not-A}$$
Therefore B,

Not both not-A and not-B
Therefore A $\lor$ B

as 'A or B'. And yet surely, we think, the hypothetical is fundamentally different from the material conditional!

So what is the solution to our difficulty? We can hardly seek a way out of the impasse by denying the validity of the counterpart arguments with a hypothetical premiss. To deny the validity of a *modus ponens* – that would be going too far! So should we embrace the other alternative and deny that a hypothetical conclusion can result from a truth-functional premiss? But that would be to run foul of the obvious fact that we can reason hypothetically from such a premiss!

Without the concept of a hypothetical variant there is no escape from this quandary. For without this concept we are unable to grasp how an argument of the form

> Not both p and not-q
> Therefore if p then q

can be valid without being valid under this form. (As, of course, we *are* unable to grasp how an argument of the form

> Not both p and not-q
> Therefore $p \rightarrow q$

can be valid without being valid under this form!) However, once we realise that an argument of this form is simply valid under the form it has as a hypothetical variant of an argument of the form

> Not both p and not-q
> p
> Therefore q

– a form which the argument schema cannot represent – the difficulty vanishes and it becomes clear that the integrity of the hypothetical as a form of statement that is logically incommensurate with the material conditional is not compromised by countenancing the validity of the counterpart arguments.

23. With the realisation that such different forms of argument as (iv), (v) and (vii) all share the same logical form, we found it necessary to draw a distinction within the general notion of the form of an argument between what we called the argument form and the root form (*vide* §16). In contrast with the account we gave of the argument form of an argument, which depends on how its limbs are introduced – whether they are asserted or introduced as hypotheses or theses – the root form was explained as that which is common to an argument and its various dialectical variants. As the chosen name suggests, it is determined by the *principle* of the argument, which finds expression in a general hypothetical. So the root form of the disjunctive syllogism and its

different variants, both hypothetical and thetical, is the form they all share as arguments with the common principle *If p or q and if not-p then q*. Accordingly, where the principle is one that belongs to logic, as it is here, the root form of an argument will be what is understood by its logical form.

A principle of inference gives expression to forms under which a proposition Q is inferable from propositions $P_1, \ldots, P_n$ and so in the case of what we have called a standard argument root form and argument form coincide. For where the premisses and conclusion of an argument are simply assertoric, the schema representing the argument form can be converted into a general hypothetical expressing the principle of the argument by introducing the premiss-schemas severally by 'if' and replacing 'therefore' by 'then'. In this way the schema that represents the argument form of the disjunctive syllogism converts into the general hypothetical that expresses the principle of that name, and the schema

> *Fa*
> *Ga*
> Therefore something (that is) *F* is *G*

which represents the argument form of

> Keynes is a Cambridge economist
> Keynes is married to a Russian ballerina
> Therefore some Cambridge economist is married to a Russian ballerina

converts into 'If *Fa* and if *Ga* then something (that is) *F* is *G*', which expresses a principle of predicate logic. If finally we may take the schema

> The (spherical) heavenly body *a* is in quadrature with the Sun
> at *t*
> Therefore *a* appears semi-circular at *t*

to represent the argument form of the physical argument, then this converts into the expression for its principle.

The distinction between argument form and root form is fundamental to logic but is everywhere overlooked. It is overlooked because we have too narrow a conception of what an argument is. We conceive essentially of an argument as a piece of discourse in which the speaker asserts one or more propositions and then asserts some further proposition on the ground of their truth, and fail to reflect – despite our common practice in drawing inferences from and to thetical and hypothetical statements – that the premisses and conclusion of an argument need not be statements that are simply assertoric. And along with this impoverished conception of an argument goes the common presumption of logicians that the logical form of an argument can *always* be represented by a schema of the argument – a presumption which the demonstration of the concept of a dialectical variant has shown to be mistaken.

It seems, in fact, that the logical form of an argument, or more generally the root form, can only be represented by a schema of the argument if the premisses and conclusion are simply assertoric. The case of an argument by *modus ponens*, where a hypothetical only occurs as a premiss, is no exception, for whilst we can represent its argument form by a schema of the argument, that schema will not translate into a general hypothetical: a clause forming a hypothetical, being one which introduces a proposition as a hypothesis, cannot itself be introduced as a hypothesis. So *a fortiori* the schema of a *modus ponens* will not translate into an expression for the principle of the argument, whatever that might be.

24. The question that must now engage our attention is the question: How is it possible that there should be different forms of argument with the same root form? In short, how is it possible that an argument should have dialectical variants? Where the difference is one of content, it goes without saying that different arguments with the same root form are possible – for with the notion of the same root form or principle we are given at the same time the possibility of different arguments with that principle – but how are we to account for the possibility of *different forms of argument* with the same root form – arguments as different in their forms as a disjunctive syllogism and its thetical and hypothetical variants? Our position here may be likened to Kant's position in his *Critique of Pure Reason*, when he enquired after the possibility of synthetic *a priori* judgements: he claimed to have shown that there are such judgements, but an explanation was required of how they were possible. In the same way, we have shown that such different forms of argument as (iv), (v) and (vii) have the same root form, which is here logical form, but we stand in need of an explanation of how this is possible.

The explanation for which we are seeking has to do with the *distributive* character of the concept of a *ground* and comes to light when we ask after the significance of the difference between a dialectical variant and the parent argument. We begin by concentrating our attention on the difference between a thetical variant and the parent argument, for, once the significance of this is understood, it is but a short step towards grasping the significance of the difference between an argument and a hypothetical variant thereof.

25. How, then, are we to describe the dialectical import of an argument in which the conclusion is a thetical statement? It is clear that in drawing a conclusion of this form you are not putting some proposition forward as true – as with a hypothetical it is the mode of assertion that is complex and not a propositional content – so *what* is the *character* of the act effected by uttering a thetical? The obvious, but at first sight puzzling, answer is that to make such

a statement is to assert the consequent of the thetical on the ground of the truth of the antecedent(s). The answer is puzzling because we are then hard pressed to understand how such a statement can itself be the conclusion of an argument.

Let us take the case of a thetical in which the consequent is inferable from the antecedent alone – say, 'Since every man loves himself, every man loves someone'. The question then is, what can distinguish this so-called statement from the argument 'Every man loves himself: therefore every man loves someone'? What can distinguish the two formations, if in using the form of words with 'since' you are asserting 'Every man loves someone' on the ground of the truth of 'Every man loves himself'? For surely this is what you are doing when you copulate the two propositions with 'therefore'!

The difficulty is resolved by distinguishing two ways of construing 'asserting Q on the ground of the truth of P', according to whether the verb has wide or narrow scope. Thus we have the description

Asserting Q, on the ground of the truth of P

where the punctuation shows that the scope of 'asserting' is confined to the opening phrase, so that the sense is

Asserting Q and doing so on the ground of the truth of P

and, as against this, we have the description in which the scope of 'asserting' extends over the whole, so that the sense is

Asserting (Q on the ground of the truth of P).

Now it is only the first description that applies to the act effected by copulating 'every man loves himself' and 'every man loves someone' with 'therefore' – the act of *inferring* the one proposition from the other. Of course, this same description applies also to the act of asserting the second proposition on its own, when the assertion is made on the (unstated) ground that every man loves himself, so to have a description that is peculiar to the argument we need something like

Asserting P and then asserting Q, on the ground of the truth of P.

The second description, on the other hand, applies to the act effected by copulating P and Q with 'since', for the wide scope of 'asserting' is needed to capture *the assertive unity* of this act – the unity which constitutes saying 'Since every man loves himself, every man loves someone' the making of a (single) statement.

26. A description, then, of the inference drawn in presenting (vii) would be

> Asserting 'Either E or Y' and then asserting 'Y' on the ground of the truth of 'not-E', on the ground of the truth of the disjunction

which, of course, only makes sense if 'asserting' at its second occurrence is read with wide scope. If, in the light of this, we now ask how it is possible that (vii) should have the same root form as (iv), it is clear what the answer must be. For it is essential to the notion of a ground that

> If the truth of P and Q serve as a ground for asserting R then the truth of P serves as a ground for asserting R on the ground of the truth of Q

where again 'asserting' at its second occurrence has wide scope. This can then be generalised, so that we have

> If the truth of Γ, P_1, . . ., P_n serve as a ground for asserting Q then the truth of Γ serve as a ground for asserting Q on the ground of the truth of P_1, . . ., P_n

where Γ is a (possibly empty) set of propositions. The limiting case in which Γ is empty provides for the case of a degenerate thetical variant.

It is this principle – this synthetic *a priori* principle as it may be called – that explains how it is possible that an argument should have thetical variants.

27. Now if a form of statement is possible in which a proposition or propositions are introduced as propositions whose truth serves as a ground for asserting another proposition then a form of statement must be possible in which a proposition or propositions are introduced as propositions whose truth *would serve* as a ground for asserting another. Such a form of statement is the hypothetical.

We have thus the concept of a *potential* ground and therewith the act, effected by the utterance of a hypothetical, of asserting one proposition on the potential ground of the truth of another, and this gives the sense in which a hypothetical asserts one proposition on the 'condition' of the truth of another. A condition, so understood, is a potential ground. Now, of course, we can only read the verb in

> Asserting Q on the potential ground of the truth of P

as having wide scope. There is no such thing as asserting a proposition and doing so on the potential ground of the truth of another! So the difference between saying 'If every man loves himself then every man loves someone' and saying 'Suppose that every man loves himself: then every man loves someone' cannot be simply assimilated to that between making the thetical statement and presenting the corresponding argument. All the same, just as you can introduce a proposition as a thesis either by asserting it or by incorporating it as the antecedent of a thetical statement, so you can introduce a proposition as a hypothesis either by explicitly framing it as such – which you do in drawing an inference from a hypothesis – or by incorporating it as the antecedent of a hypothetical statement (*vide* §10). So we have a distinction between the compound act of

> Framing the hypothesis that P is true and then asserting Q on the potential ground of the truth of P

and the unitary act of asserting one proposition on the potential ground of the truth of another, for which we use the hypothetical form of statement. It is true, of course, that you cannot draw an inference from a hypothesis and leave it there. A hypothesis is *framed* only to be discharged by some later step in the argument of which the hypothesis forms part, and so there is an incompleteness about the act effected by saying 'Suppose that every man loves himself: then no man is unloved' that is absent from that effected by uttering the corresponding hypothetical.

We have, then, the following description of the step involved in moving from an argument to a hypothetical variant thereof. If I begin by presenting (iv) but then become uncertain of the truth of the second premiss and so withdraw to (v), I move from asserting 'Either E or Y' and 'not-E' and then asserting 'Y' on the ground of their truth to

> Asserting 'Either E or Y' and then asserting 'Y' on the potential ground of the truth of 'not-E', on the ground of the truth of the disjunction.

But it is a corollary of the principle enunciated in the last section that

> If the truth of Γ, P_1, . . ., P_n serve as a ground for asserting Q then the truth of Γ serve as ground for asserting Q on the potential ground of the truth of P_1, . . ., P_n

so with this we have the explanation of how it is possible that an argument should have hypothetical variants.

28. Whilst the notion of asserting one proposition on the ground of the truth of another is unexceptionable, a difficulty may be felt about that of asserting a proposition on the *potential* ground of the truth of another. For since it goes without saying that the consequent of a hypothetical is not asserted, what can be the significance of describing the act effected by its utterance in these terms? How is the use of 'asserting' in the description to be justified? To

answer this question and win recognition for the notion of asserting something on a potential ground, we need to understand how the structure of a hypothetical – its grammatical make-up as a statement formed with a subordinating conjunction in which the subordinate clause(s) lie outside the scope of the main verb – bears upon the linguistic act effected by its utterance.

29. To this end we introduce the concept of the *Mood* of a sentence. In the sense required by logic, a sentence is a formation by whose utterance, independent of context, a unitary linguistic act is effected. (Which is not to say, of course, that the *identity* of a sentence may not depend upon context, as it does, for instance, when it contains an anaphoric pronoun.) Accordingly, there must be a property associated with a sentence which identifies the linguistic act effected by its utterance, and it is this property, essential to a sentence, that we designate by the word 'Mood', using a capital letter. The Mood of a sentence, we shall say, *portrays* the act effected by its utterance.

The Mood of a sentence will often be determined by the inflection of the main verb – by the *grammatical* mood of the sentence – but this is by no means always the case and there are, in particular, sentences where the inflection of the main verb is only *part* of what determines Mood. Amongst these are sentences containing a subordinate clause that lies outside the scope of the main verb. There is no question but that the sentences 'Every man loves someone' and 'Since every man loves himself, every man loves someone' have the same mood, grammatically speaking, since the main verb of each bears the indicative inflection, but plainly their Moods are different. The Mood of the first, which is determined by its grammatical mood as an indicative sentence, portrays the act of asserting a proposition *tout court*, and we have called a sentence with this Mood simply assertoric (*vide* §4). The Mood of the second, however, portrays the act of asserting one proposition on the ground of the truth of another and so cannot be determined by its grammatical mood alone. Its Mood, we may say, is assertoric, but it is not simply assertoric.

It will be convenient to speak of the *mark* by which Mood is conveyed. Thus where the Mood of a sentence is determined by the inflection of the main verb, we shall say that this grammatical feature is the mark by which the Mood of the sentence is conveyed. Where, however, such verbal inflection bears upon, but does not determine, the Mood of the sentence, we shall say that it is part of the mark by which its Mood is conveyed. The marks by which Mood is conveyed are multifarious and include, in the case of the spoken language, such things as gesture, intonation and facial expression. Our concern as logicians is primarily with the written or printed language and so with marks of Mood that can be recognised from the printed page.

30. The concept of assertoric Mood simpliciter is closely related to what Frege understands by 'assertoric force', which he describes as 'closely bound

up with the indicative mood in main clauses'.[11] However, it is important to notice that Frege's concept is different from the present one in that a sentence carries assertoric force only if it is uttered 'seriously' and the speaker is not, say, reading from a book or acting a part or telling a story, and so on. This indeed is a reason for preferring the concept of Mood to that of force and it is surprising that Frege, who was so concerned in his investigations 'always to separate sharply the psychological from the logical',[12] should have operated with such an impure concept as that of assertoric force. For whilst a sentence will not express an assertion unless it is uttered 'seriously', logic can only take account of that property of a sentence in virtue of which it expresses an assertion *if* it is uttered seriously. That property is what we are calling the (simple) assertoric Mood of a sentence.

31. Recognition of a sentence as a formation to which a Mood is essential underlies the grammatical distinction between a sentence and the clause that forms it. The clause that forms the sentence 'Every man loves someone' is present in the sentence 'It is true that every man loves someone', where it is introduced by the propositional prefix 'it is true that', but a Mood belongs only to the whole sentence, not to the clause, as indeed is shown by the fact that it appears here in dependent form. Frege capitalises on the distinction between clause and sentence by introducing as a mark of assertoric Mood a sign *that is not a part of speech*, with the consequence that an assertoric sentence in his ideography is not formed by a grammatical clause at all. Thus the Fregean sentence '⊢ (that) every man loves someone', which begins with the assertion-sign, contains the proposition 'every man loves someone' as a dependent clause in common with the sentence 'It is the true that every man loves someone', but since there is no clause running '⊢ (that) every man loves someone', it stands out that the formation with the assertion-sign is a sentence. By contrast, the sentence with the prefix 'it is true' is formed by the clause which appears at a second remove in the sentence 'It is true that it is true that every man loves someone'.

Do we not have an analogous formation to the Fregean sentence in the case of the sentence 'Suppose that every man loves himself'? Here we are comparing the word 'suppose', which operates in the sentence as a mark of what might be called the *hypothetical* Mood – the Mood which portrays the act of framing a hypothesis – to the sign '⊢'. For although it is true that the mood of the verbal prefix counts as grammatically imperative, the sentence is not formed by an imperative clause. It is not like the sentence 'Imagine you are seeing a red patch', and we cannot say, for example, 'When you have concluded the present argument, suppose that every man loves himself', as we can say 'When your eyes are closed, imagine you are seeing a red patch'.

In the light of the foregoing, it appears that Wittgenstein's comment on the assertion-sign when he likens its function to that of the full-stop, saying that 'it marks the *beginning of the sentence*', fails to take the measure of Frege's conception.[13] It seems indeed wide of the mark. One may agree with his statement that the assertion-sign 'distinguishes the whole period from a clause within the period', but it does not accomplish this through marking the beginning of the sentence, as the full-stop marks the end. It accomplishes it through generating a sentence that is not formed by a grammatical clause. In fact, the assertion-sign no more marks the beginning of a sentence than does the word 'suppose'. On the contrary, it begins, and is thus *part of*, a sentence.

Through transcending the resources of natural language, and introducing a special sign as a mark of assertoric Mood, Frege has devised a wholly new form for a sentence asserting a proposition – a form which marks it out as a sentence. Nevertheless, in a language modelled on Frege's *Begriffsschrift*, where a proposition only occurs as asserted if it is introduced by an assertion-sign, there would exist no assertoric sentences containing a subordinating conjunction of the type that generates a thetical or hypothetical statement. For where, in such a language, could we place the assertion-sign in constructing such a sentence? There would, for instance, be no thetical sentences, since neither the formation '⊢ since every man loves himself, every man loves someone' nor the formation 'Since every man loves himself, ⊢ every man loves someone' is a possible sentence. Obviously not the first, because the assertion-sign can only introduce a proposition, but not the second either, because the words with the assertion-sign attached do not constitute a grammatical clause.

32. In the present connection it is instructive to consider a criticism that the early Wittgenstein made of Frege's view of a proposition as a complex name. We may remember that in his later writings Frege came to regard a proposition in this way, and it is suggested in the *Tractatus* that what made it possible for him to do this is that 'in a printed proposition a propositional sign does not appear essentially different from a word'[14] – as it would, so the *Tractatus* thinks, if it were put together out of objects such as tables and chairs, instead of written signs. Here the idea is that such a way of forming a propositional sign would reveal the pictorial nature of the proposition – its *Bildhaftigkeit* – but whatever one may think of this, the suggestion that Frege was able to regard a proposition as he did because of its usual appearance in print is surely mistaken. What is significant about a proposition is that, unlike a sentence, it does not have a Mood *as such*, and it is only because we can no more ascribe a Mood to the clauses of a truth-functional sentence than to the terms of a complex numerical designation that he was able to compare, say, the disjunction 'Black has lost his queen or White has lost a bishop' with a designation such as '$3^2 + 5^4$' and view the truth/falsity of the disjunction and its clauses as *values* of these expressions. With this comparison, he is then able to say that as the numerical value of the complex numerical designation is determined by the numerical values of the summands, so the *truth*-value of the disjunction is determined by the truth-values of the disjuncts. True, this of itself does not amount to regarding a proposition as a singular term

designating one of its values, but unless the comparison with a numerical expression were possible he would not have been able to take the further step of treating a proposition – *not* a sentence! – as a complex name.[15]

There is indeed a certain irony in Wittgenstein's response to Frege's conception of a proposition, for it is only because a proposition does not have a Mood as such that he is able to present his rival account of it as a picture or model of reality. No Mood belongs to a picture or model, and the comparison implied at 3.1431

'The essence of a propositional sign is very clearly seen if we imagine one composed of three-dimensional[16] objects (such as tables, chairs and books) instead of written signs. Then the spatial arrangement of these things will express the sense of the proposition'

between say, 'Leeds is north of London' and a model in which the spatial relation between a chair and table represents the geographical relation between Leeds and London seems intelligible to us only because we distinguish between the proposition, to which a Mood is not essential, and the sentence. It would be patently absurd to speak in this way of the 'essence' of the formation '⊢ Leeds is north of London', and *by the same token* it would be absurd to speak in this way of the essence of the *sentence* 'Leeds is north of London'.

A natural objection to this account of the proposition is that it is hard to see how the proposition could then enjoy its pre-eminent role in the *Tractatus* as the only complex sign with sense, since on such a view no propositional sign would then *say* anything. The thesis of 3.1431 is developed at 3.1432 with the remark that in place of

The complex sign *aRb* says that *a* stands to *b* in the relation *R*

we should put

That '*a*' stands to '*b*' in a certain relation says *that aRb*

which means that in place of

The complex sign 'Leeds is north of London' says that Leeds stands to London in the relation *north of*

we should put

That 'Leeds' stands to 'London' in a certain relation says *that* Leeds is north of London.

But should we? The transition from the one statement to the other is beguiling, but the verb 'says' in the last sentence is surely out of place. For if, as the *Tractatus* teaches, a proposition is a picture or model of reality and the relation that is set up between the names in the sign 'Leeds is north of London' is significant in the way that the relation between the elements of a model is significant, then the above should be amended to read something like

> *That* 'Leeds' stands to 'London' in a certain relation signifies that Leeds is north of London

or, dispensing with the *that*-clause

> *That* 'Leeds' stands to 'London' in a certain relation represents Leeds as being north of London.

Now, unlike 'says', the verbs in these two sentences do not induce an oblique context and the content of what is signified or represented can be specified in different ways. Thus a relation which represents Leeds as being north of London at the same time represents the capital of the United Kingdom as being south of the largest city in Yorkshire. So how can this account give the *essence* of a propositional sign, when it is the essence of such a sign that it *says* something?

33. Frege's later conception of the proposition, along with the rival conception offered by the *Tractatus*, suffer from the same defect. For whilst they both exploit the fact that no Mood belongs to a proposition as such, they fail to provide for the fact that a proposition, unlike a complex name or model, can form a sentence. Indeed if this were not so, how could we speak of a proposition as saying something? It is the peculiarity of a proposition that as an *expression for* something, albeit a truth-value, no Mood belongs to it, any more than a Mood belongs to an expression for a number, yet as an expression for a *truth-value*, it has the structure of a grammatical clause – a clause, moreover, that can form, in the sense of being coterminous with, a sentence in which it is itself put forward as an expression for the truth-value of truth. With the introduction of his assertion-sign Frege devised in his *Begriffsschrift* a formal language in which a proposition only appears as a dependent clause and so never forms a sentence, but in our ordinary language, which is without an assertion-sign, the only way to form a sentence that is simply assertoric is with an expression for a truth-value, and this entails the occurrence of propositions as *main* clauses. What we have now to recognise is that although no Mood belongs to a proposition as such, a Mood does belong to it when it is a main clause – given the right conception of such a clause. If we think of the main verb in a proposition as the nerve which transmits the assertoric impulse, then this nerve will be active when the proposition forms a sentence.

What is important for our present concern, however, is to recognise that it is also active when a proposition is the main clause *of* a sentence. So a Mood belongs to a proposition when it is the consequent of a hypothetical.

34. It will no doubt be conceded that a Mood belongs to the main clause of a thetical sentence, or, again, to the main clause of a concessive sentence, just because these are asserted clauses. But to the main clause of a hypothetical? Here it is natural to object that no Mood can belong to the main clause of 'If every man loves himself, every man loves someone', on the ground that we do not assert this clause in making the hypothetical statement. But the objection is mistaken. For although we may be *assured* that a Mood belongs to the main clause of 'Since every man loves himself, every man loves someone' and 'Although every man loves himself, no man is free from despair', because their main clauses are asserted, it is in virtue of their status *as main clauses*, whether asserted or not, that a Mood belongs to them.

Mood, as we have introduced the concept, is the hallmark of a sentence: it belongs essentially to a sentence as a formation by whose utterance, independent of context, a linguistic act is effected. This means that we can only be justified in operating with the notion of the Mood of a proposition if it somehow imports that of the Mood of a sentence associated with it. So if it is to be ascribed to a proposition, not only when it forms a sentence – is a main clause coterminous with a sentence – but also when it is the main clause of a sentence, this can only be so in virtue of the Mood of the sentence itself. Using 'sub' to stand in for a subordinating conjunction, it will be because a sentence of the general form *Sub p_1, . . ., p_n, q* has such and such a (complex) Mood that the *q*-clause has a Mood.

If therefore a Mood belongs to a proposition as the main clause of a sentence, this does not entail that the act effected by the utterance of the main clause when it forms a sentence – the act, namely, of asserting a proposition – must be part of the act effected by the utterance of the sentence of which it is part, but only that a *description* of the latter act must allude to the former. Hence we cannot infer that if a Mood belongs to the main clause of 'Since every man loves himself, every man loves someone', then the (complex) act effected by the utterance of the sentence must contain the act effected by the utterance of 'every man loves someone' when this forms a sentence, for *whether that is so can only depend upon the Mood of the thetical sentence itself.* We can only infer that if a Mood does belong to the main clause here, then a description of the act effected by the utterance of the thetical must allude to the act effected by the utterance of this clause when it forms a sentence. True, we know that the act effected by the utterance of the thetical does contain that of asserting 'every man loves someone', and this, of course, will be evident from the description of the act, but we must allow for the possibility that there should be a complex act whose description alludes to the act of asserting a proposition, although it does not itself contain such an act. Here, it will be understood, we have the hypothetical in mind. It goes without saying that you do not assert 'every man loves someone' in uttering the sentence 'If every man loves himself then every man loves someone', but the burden of our argument is that the Mood of this sentence nevertheless portrays an act whose description alludes to the act of asserting that proposition.

As we might say, the Mood of a sentence is *autonomous*, but not that of a clause.

35. Given, then, that a Mood belongs to a proposition only in virtue of the Mood of the sentence of which it is a clause, under what conditions does it so belong? Plainly the answer must be that

> A Mood belongs to a proposition P as a clause of a sentence S if the mark that conveys the Mood of P when it forms a sentence is part of the mark that conveys the Mood of S.

Letting now S be a sentence of the general form $Sub\ p_1, \ldots, p_n, q$ and P the main clause, it clearly follows that P has a Mood. For the main verb of P is at the same time the main verb of S and so the (indicative) inflection of the verb must bear upon the Mood of S. But this inflection is the mark that conveys the Mood of P when it forms a sentence. So the mark that conveys the Mood of P when it forms a sentence is part of the mark that conveys that Mood of S. It cannot be the whole of the mark, since the subordinate clause(s) of S lie outside the scope of the main verb. This being so, the character of the subordinating conjunction must also bear upon the Mood of S. But now it goes without saying that the Mood of a hypothetical cannot be the same as that of a thetical, or the Mood of either the same as that of a concessive sentence. We therefore reach the conclusion that a sentence of this general form is, as we may put it, φ-*wise assertoric*, where the value of 'φ' depends on the particular conjunction by which the sentence is generated.

The complexity of the Mood reflects the complexity of the act portrayed by it, and as the Mood of a thetical sentence portrays the act of asserting one proposition on the ground of the truth of another (others), so the Mood of a hypothetical portrays the act of asserting one proposition on the potential ground of the truth of another (others). Accordingly, the Mood of a thetical might be called the *grounded assertoric Mood* and the Mood of a hypothetical the *potentially grounded assertoric Mood*.

Of course, we can hardly speak of the mark that conveys the Mood of the main clause of 'If every man were to love himself then every man would love someone' when it forms a sentence, but we have to bear in mind that the only difference between this statement and the corresponding statement in the indicative is that the wording with 'were' and 'would' signifies, as the indicative mood does not, that the hypothetical is one that will accommodate expression of the speaker's belief that it is not true that every man loves himself or, again, expression of his belief that it is true that every man loves someone. The indicative mood can always be projected into the subjunctive mood when a hypothetical is of this character. So we recognise that whether we use the indicative form or the subjunctive form, we are making a statement in the potentially grounded assertoric Mood, as indeed shows itself in the possibility of expanding the statement above into 'If it were true that every man loves himself then it would be true that every man loves someone' (*vide* §8).

A conjunction that helps to convey the Mood of sentences formed by its means might be called a *conjunction of Mood*.[17]

36. In addition to subordinating conjunctions of Mood, there are conjunctions of Mood in which the conjoined clauses are *co-ordinate* with one another. With conjunctions of this type the co-ordinated clauses each count as main clauses, the clause or clauses preceding the conjunction because they form sentences, and the clause following because it is introduced by such a conjunction. If we do not count the resultant formations themselves as sentences, that is because they already contain at least one sentence, so that we can only speak of 'the' act effected by their utterance by allowing ourselves the fiction of a compound act. It was essentially for this reason that we distinguished in §25 between the argument 'Every man loves himself: therefore every man loves someone' and the corresponding thetical statement. Since the formation with 'therefore' begins with an assertoric sentence, an assertive act is *already* effected by uttering the opening clause alone, which is why 'asserting' has narrow scope in the description of the argument as 'asserting one proposition on the ground of the truth of another'. Likewise the formation 'Suppose that every man loves himself: then every man loves someone' begins with a sentence, which distinguishes it from the corresponding hypothetical statement, only here you could not utter the opening sentence and leave matters there, drawing no inference from the hypothesis expressed, as you could, of course, utter the sentence in the formation with 'therefore' without going on to draw an inference from your assertion. Nevertheless, it is the fact that it begins with a sentence – a sentence in the hypothetical Mood – that distinguishes it, along with the argument formation, from a statement.

Now we may think of a sentence of the form *Sub p, q* as resulting from a formation of the form *S co q* by a process of subordination. In this process the co-ordinating conjunction represented by 'co' gives way to a subordinating conjunction and the clause that formed the original sentence becomes subordinate to the *q*-clause, which remains as a main clause. In this way a thetical statement results from a formation with 'therefore', a hypothetical statement from a formation beginning 'Suppose that . . . ' and a statement of the form 'Although *p, q*' from a formation running '*p* but *q*'.

Since a formation containing such a co-ordinating conjunction already contains a sentence, we can hardly deny it a Mood, but here the Mood will be conveyed by the marks which convey the Mood of S and the q-clause, together with the particular conjunction involved. Thus the Mood of the first of the above formations, which portrays the compound act of asserting one proposition and then asserting another on the ground of its truth, is conveyed by the indicative inflection of each of the two verbs together with the conjunction 'therefore', and the Mood of the second, which portrays the compound act of framing a proposition as a hypothesis and then asserting another on the potential ground of its truth, is conveyed by the prefix 'suppose that' and the indicative inflection of the verb of the q-clause together with the conjunction 'then'.

37. Our thesis is that a Mood belongs to a proposition when it is a main clause, given the right conception of such a clause. The qualification is needed to provide for the case of a proposition occurring as the clause of a disjunction or truth-functional statement generally. No Mood belongs to a proposition in such a position and to assume otherwise would be to assimilate a logical constant – a conjunction that contributes to determining the truth-conditions of propositions formed by its means – to a conjunction of Mood. But in contradistinction to the grammar of the *Begriffsschrift* with its possession of an assertion-sign, it is a feature of the grammar of our language that it allows us to form a *sentence* by completing a sign for a truth-function, so that we do not merely form a complex expression for a truth-value out of simpler ones by writing 'White has lost a bishop or Black has lost a queen', we actually say something – as we say something when we write 'White has lost a bishop but Black has lost his queen', where we have two bona fide main clauses – and this makes it look as if the sign for disjunction is used to 'disjoin one assertion with another', as the conjunction 'but' is used to make one assertion in contrast with another. In fact, however, the clauses in a disjunction should be thought of as co-ordinate clauses in *one* main clause, as would be evident if we employed the propositional prefix of §5 and formed the disjunction with 'it is true that', enclosing the whole of what follows in brackets to show the scope of the prefix. With the *but*-formation, on the other hand, the scope of the prefix could only embrace the first clause, since this already forms an assertoric sentence.

Of course, the difference between the disjunctive sentence and the formation with 'but' comes out in a number of ways and we are not misled by their surface likeness. In particular, the former can be expanded into 'Either White has lost a bishop or Black has lost his queen', whereas the latter does not admit of a similar expansion. We cannot introduce a correlative sign before the first clause of the formation with 'but' because, as we have remarked, that clause forms a sentence and so you have already said something before you have introduced the second clause.

It is worth noting that the word 'and' is used not only as a truth-functional connective but also as a conjunction of Mood. We have to distinguish between the *sentence* 'White has lost a bishop and Black has lost his queen', which we could write with our prefix as 'It is true both that White has lost a bishop and Black has lost his queen', and the formation that begins with the sentence 'White has lost a bishop' and then, using the word 'and', conjoins with it the clause 'Black has lost his queen'. In uttering the sentence, we assert the conjunction of two propositions; in uttering the described formation, we assert one proposition and join the assertion of a second proposition to it. This compound act is thus to be compared with that effected by uttering the corresponding formation with 'but', for when I say 'White has lost a bishop but Black has lost his queen', I also conjoin two assertions, only this is not a complete description of what I do. I am making the one assertion in contrast with the other. I conjoin, one might say, two assertions in the contrastive mode.

38. Since the conjunction that generates a hypothetical is a conjunction of Mood, it follows that a clause that forms a hypothetical cannot occur un-asserted in ordinary speech – that is, where it is not being quoted or used to report what someone asserts or believes and so on – and this, of course, marks it off from a clause that forms a sentence whose Mood is simply assertoric. Thus if you utter a clause that forms a hypothetical and the context is one of ordinary speech then you will be asserting one proposition on the potential ground of the truth of another – always provided, of course, that you are speaking seriously. In short, you will be making a hypothetical statement.

There is nothing remarkable in this contention, any more than there is in the contention that you cannot make an utterance of the form *Suppose p: then q* outside quotation marks without drawing an inference from a supposition. Indeed since a hypothetical can be seen as resulting from such an inferential formation by a process of subordination, the first contention follows from the second.

Since the Mood of a clause that forms a hypothetical is thus *inalienable*, it follows that we cannot read

> Suppose Keynes is married to a Russian ballerina: then if Keynes is a Cambridge economist, some Cambridge economist is married to a Russian ballerina

as we should read, say

> Suppose Yeats suffered his last serious illness in 1938: then before Eliot composed *Little Gidding* he was dead

but as with

> Suppose Keynes is married to Russian ballerina: then since Keynes is a
> Cambridge economist, some Cambridge economist is married to a
> Russian ballerina

have to take the subordinate clause as lying outside the scope of the
inferential particle (*vide* §9).

Again, it follows that a clause that forms a hypothetical cannot occur
within the scope of a truth-functional connective. So we might well balk at

> If White has advanced his queen then he is in danger of losing a rook or
> if he has moved his king then he is in danger of losing a bishop

and seek a propositional reading for the disjoined clauses, whereas we should,
of course, have no difficulty in understanding

> If White has advanced his queen then he is in danger of losing his rook
> but if he has moved his king then he is in danger of losing his bishop.

We could, as it were, put the thesis that the Mood of such a clause is
inalienable to the test by comparing

> > If White has advanced his queen then he is in danger of losing
> > his rook or his bishop
> > Therefore if White has advanced his queen then he is in danger of losing
> > his rook or if he has advanced his queen then he is danger of
> > losing his bishop

with the corresponding argument of the form

$$p \to (q \text{ or } r)$$
$$\text{Therefore } (p \to q) \text{ or } (p \to r).$$

There is nothing paradoxical in the argument that concludes with a statement
disjoining one material conditional with another, which is clearly valid, but if
anyone argued in the first way would it not be *as if* he were uncertain which of
two inferences to draw? Would it not be as if he were uncertain whether to
draw the inference

> > If White has advanced his queen then he is in danger of losing
> > his rook or his bishop
> > Therefore if White has advanced his queen then he is in danger his losing
> > his rook,

or the inference

> If White has advanced his queen then he is in danger of losing his rook or his bishop
> Therefore if White has advanced his queen then he is in danger of losing his bishop

both of which are invalid?

39. In this connection it is instructive to note that when Frege provides readings for the formulas of his *Begriffsschrift* he invariably renders the main occurrence of his conditional stroke by 'if . . . then', whilst subordinate occurrences attract a variety of different readings. For instance, the reading he gives to illustrate the principle of contraposition, which in our more familiar notation will be represented by '⊦ $(p \rightarrow q) \rightarrow (\neg q \rightarrow \neg p)$', is 'If from the circumstance that M is alive his breathing can be inferred, then from the circumstance that he is not breathing his death can be inferred'.[18] One may find this puzzling, for the argument by contraposition is not the argument

> From the circumstance that M is alive his breathing can be inferred
> Therefore from the circumstance that he is not breathing his death can be inferred

in which the premiss and conclusion are statements whose Mood is simply assertoric, but the argument

> If M is alive then he is breathing
> Therefore if he is not breathing then he is not alive

and the principle of contraposition is exemplified by

> If Yeats died before 1940 then he was outlived by Eliot
> Therefore if he was not outlived by Eliot then he did not die before 1940

where the consequent of the opening hypothetical is not inferable from its antecedent, no less than by the argument above. However, the impossibility of incorporating a clause that forms a hypothetical statement as itself the antecedent or consequent of a hypothetical means that Frege is not able to frame a hypothetical statement *corresponding to* the argument by contraposition and so is reduced to an inconsistent reading for the main and subordinate occurrences of his conditional stroke.

Of course, language is capable of the most varied twists and turns in its striving for ellipsis, and one may construct a sentence running 'If if M is alive then he is breathing then if he is not breathing then he is not alive', but here it will only be the outer 'if' that introduces a hypothesis. What then makes it natural to identify this hypothesis with the hypothesis that from the circumstance that M is alive his breathing can be inferred is the fact that the hypothetical 'If M is alive then he is breathing' would normally be given a strong reading as one in which the consequent is introduced as a proposition that is inferable from the antecedent. So it is easy to see that in this spirit one might even construct a disjunctive sentence of the *apparent* form *if p then q or if r then s* – a disjunctive sentence whose clauses have the wording of a hypothetical – in a case where the associated hypotheticals would command such a reading. In this way, one obtains a neat and economical expression for what would otherwise be expressed by a statement running 'That *q* is inferable from that *p* or that *s* is inferable from that *r*'.

40. It follows from the foregoing that it would be a mistake to think that we could introduce brackets into a hypothetical like 'If the card on top is an ace then if it's not the ace of spades then it's the ace of diamonds' and construe it as 'If the card on top is an ace then (if it's not the ace of spades then it's the ace of diamonds)'. Here we do not have a hypothetical whose main clause is itself a clause that forms a hypothetical, but a hypothetical with two antecedents, only these are introduced stepwise and not in co-ordination. So an argument running

> If the card on top is an ace then if it's not the ace of spades
> then it's the ace of diamonds
> The card on top is an ace
> Therefore if it's not the ace of spades then it's the ace of diamonds

is not a *modus ponens* strictly speaking, but an incomplete or interrupted *modus ponens*. In executing a *modus ponens* proper both the hypotheses in the major premiss would have to be discharged, in order then to be able to assert its consequent.

Lewis Carroll's familiar paradox of the barber shop trades on the assumption that what looks like a hypothetical of the form *If p then (if q then r)* really is such. In his ornamental version of the paradox we are asked to imagine a barber shop that is run by three men called Carr, Allen and Brown. We are given that the shop is never left unattended and that Allen never goes out without Brown, and so at any time we are in a position to assert both 'If Carr is (now) out then if Allen is out then Brown is not out' and 'If Allen is out then Brown is out'. The reasoning of the paradox is then that since what Carroll calls the sub-hypothetical 'If Allen is out then Brown is not out' is incompatible with the hypothetical 'If Allen is out then Brown is out', it may be inferred that Carr is not out.[19] From what we have been given, however, it is evident that we may only infer that either Carr or Allen is not out. Here it is clear that that argument cannot so much as get started if the complex hypothetical has both 'Carr is out' and 'Allen is out' as antecedents, and with this understanding the true state of affairs immediately asserts itself. As for the issue of incompatibility, the so-called incompatibility of hypotheticals is hypothetical incompatibility, which is to say that no contradiction is inferable from 'If Allen is out then Brown is out' and 'If Allen is out then Brown is not out' by themselves, but only from these statements together with the statement asserting their common antecedent.

If we thought that the conclusion of

> It is not the case that Carr and Allen and Brown are out
> Therefore if Carr is out then if Allen is out then Brown is not out

were a hypothetical with 'Carr is out' as its only antecedent, we should be at a loss to say what its logical form was. For with such a reading we could not identify any argument as the parent argument. We could not recognise it as a hypothetical variant of the argument

> It is not the case that C and A and B
> C
> A
> Therefore not-B

for this would require that its conclusion have both 'C' and 'A' as antecedents, but then neither could we recognise

> It is not the case that C and A and B
> C
> Therefore if A then not-B

as its parent, as we recognise

> It is not the case that C and A and B
> C
> Therefore A → not-B

as the parent of

> It is not the case that C and A and B
> Therefore if C then A → not-B.

For the argument from the paradox, being one with a hypothetical as conclusion, is not itself the parent of any variant, but one of the seven hypothetical variants of the (standard) argument with the three premisses 'It is not the case that C and A and B', 'C' and 'A'.

41. Athough 'If C then if A then not-B' and 'If C and if A then not-B' are one and the same hypothetical, there may nevertheless be a point in framing a hypothetical that has multiple antecedents with these arranged stepwise rather than in co-ordination, as we can see if we consider how we might read proofs in natural deduction format. As is well known, Gentzen had the idea of formalising proof in logic by allowing for the introduction of hypotheses and to this end distinguished two types of rules of inference: (schematic) rules under which inferences can be drawn from propositions introduced as hypotheses and (thematic) rules under which, given the validity of such an inference or inferences from hypotheses, such and such another inference is valid. With application of rules of the second type hypotheses introduced at earlier stages are 'discharged'.[20]

Following our convention of using 'A' and 'B' as dummy propositions, we may illustrate how the same hypothetical can be thus framed in different ways by considering how we might read a proof of the sequent '$\neg$(A & B), A $\vdash$ $\neg$B', which in Gentzen's lay-out will look like

$$\frac{\dfrac{A \quad B}{A \text{ \& } B} \qquad \neg(A \text{ \& } B)}{\neg B}$$

Here the propositions with no lines above them are introduced as hypotheses; the transition from 'A' and 'B' to 'A & B' is licensed by the (schematic) rule of adjunction and the consequent transition from 'A' and '$\neg$(A & B)' to '$\neg$B', by which the hypothesis 'B' is discharged, is licensed by the (thematic) rule of *reductio ad absurdum*. To interpret the tree as a piece of living reasoning, it is natural to introduce the propositions assumed as hypotheses by 'if', which gives

If A and if B then both A and B
Therefore if not both A and B and if A then not-B

where 'therefore' marks the application of the rule by which 'B' is discharged. That is to say, this is the wording we obtain if we introduce the hypotheses 'not both A and B' and 'A' in co-ordination with each other, but we may prefer the wording

If A and if B then both A and B
Therefore if not both A and B then if A then not-B

because it gives pride of place to the new hypothesis 'not both A and B' and does not introduce it on a level with 'A', which has already been introduced as a hypothesis in the premiss.

We can point up the radical difference in role between 'if' and '$\rightarrow$' by considering how we should read the extension of the above tree that results from making an application of the rule of conditional proof and discharging the hypothesis 'A'. In this way we obtain the tree

$$\frac{\dfrac{A \quad B}{A \,\&\, B} \qquad \neg(A \,\&\, B)}{\dfrac{\neg B}{A \to \neg B}}$$

which is a proof of the sequent '$\neg(A \,\&\, B) \vdash (A \to \neg B)$'. If we now introduce the hypotheses in co-ordination throughout but render the concluding proposition by 'if A then not-B', so that the whole reads

> If A and if B then both A and B
> Therefore if not both A and B and if A then not-B
> Therefore if not both A and B then if A then not-B

then, despite the difference of wording, the second 'therefore' will not introduce a further step and we shall be merely marking logical time. We have to show in our reading that the rule of conditional proof introduces a *new* logical constant into the proof, albeit one for which it seems that there is no answering conjunction in the vernacular.

So a proof of the general sequent '$\neg(p \,\&\, q) \vdash (p \to \neg q)$' might read

> If p and if q then both p and q
> Therefore if not both p and q and if p then not-q
> Therefore if not both p and q then p *arrow* not-q

where '*arrow*' is used as a makeshift reading for '$\to$'. Here we have first an inference from the principle of adjunction to the principle of *modus ponendo tollens* and then an inference from the latter to the principle under which we may infer a material conditional from the negation of a conjunction. If the ideal of a proof *in* logic is that premisses and conclusion should themselves be principles of logic then with such a reading it stands out that a proof by natural deduction has the architectonic of such a proof.

42. It is sometimes said that in a formalisation of logic by natural deduction we dispense with axioms and have only rules of inferences. But this is misleading. The difference between the formalisation of propositional logic proposed by Gentzen and the 'axiomatic' formalisation found in Frege's *Begriffsschrift* is not that in the latter we have both axioms and rules of inference, whereas in the former we have only rules of inference, but that in the latter the axioms are forms of logically true *proposition*, with inferences drawn therefrom in accordance with the (schematic) rule of detachment, whereas in the former

the axioms are themselves rules of logical inference, with inferences drawn therefrom in accordance with (thematic) rules such as that of *reductio ad absurdum*.

Expressed in these terms, the difference between the two systems is seen to stem from a difference in the *Mood* of their axioms. But beguiled by Frege's account of his project in devising 'a formal language for pure thought', this may easily escape notice. For he thinks of the system in the *Begriffsschrift* as articulating what he calls 'laws of thought' and so he speaks, for example, of the pair of axioms '$\vdash p \to \neg\,\neg p$' and '$\vdash (p \to q) \to (\neg q \to \neg p)$' as expressing 'fundamental laws of negation'.[21] And reading this, we naturally think, What can these laws be but principles of logical inference? It seems obvious, however, that no statement asserting a tautology can exemplify a principle of inference. To take the law relating to double negation, what is called such can only be the principle under which the double negation of a proposition is inferable from that proposition, and this finds expression in the general hypothetical 'If p then $\neg\,\neg p$'. There is no room in its expression for a logical constant other than '$\neg$'. As for the second of the 'laws of negation', this can only be the law under which a hypothetical can be contraposed – a law which our enquiry has yet to formulate. There is, of course, the law relating to the contraposition of a material conditional, but this again finds expression in the general hypothetical 'If $p \to q$ then $\neg q \to \neg p$', where the sign '$\to$' is confined to the body of the principle.

Amongst the laws of propositional logic there is what is called the principle of tautology – the principle under which, as a limiting case, any proposition is inferable from itself. This likewise finds expression in the hypothetical 'If p then p', not in the formula '$\vdash p \to p$', which imports a logical constant. A statement exemplifying the *principle* of tautology is not itself a tautology!

Having characterised proof in logic as 'a mechanical expedient to facilitate the recognition of tautologies in complicated cases', the *Tractatus* goes on 'It is clear from the start that the logical proof of a proposition that has sense (*sinnvoller Satz*) and a proof *in* logic must be two entirely different things'.[22] But should we not rather say that the logical proof of a *proposition*, whether it has sense or not, and the proof *in* logic must be two quite different things?

43. If it is true that the method of framing proofs by natural deduction conforms to the ideal of what proof in logic should be, still this is not to say that to every valid sequent of propositional logic there corresponds a *principle* of logical inference, and indeed there seems no way of devising a calculus in which all and only those valid sequents are provable that correspond to principles of inference. We know that a sequent of propositional logic counts as valid just in case there is no assignment of truth-values to the propositional letters under which the formula or formulas to the left of the gate come out true but not the formula to the right, and so there are

infinitely many valid sequents that do not correspond to principles of inference.

An obvious example of such is the trivial sequent '$p, q \vdash q$'. We recognise *If p and if q then p and q* and *If p and q then p* as principles of inference, but we do not thereby recognise *If p and if q then p* as such. There is no principle under which a proposition is inferable from a pair of propositions of which it is a member. Another example is the familiar sequent '$p, \neg p \vdash q$'. We recognise *If p then either p or q* and *If p or q and if not-p then q* as principles of inference, but we do not thereby recognise *If p and if not-p then q* as such. There is no principle under which an arbitrary proposition is inferable from contradictory propositions.

We may compare the expression 'is inferable from' with that of 'can be moved from ... to ...', as this might be used in speaking of the moves allowed to the pieces on a chess board. Thus, since the bishop moves diagonally, there is no rule under which the king's bishop can be moved from KB1 to KB5, but we might say all the same that it can be moved from the one position to the other, because there is a way of getting from the one position to the other in accordance with the rules of the game. We may, for example, move the bishop first from KB1 to Q3 and then from Q3 to KB5. Similarly, there is no principle under which 'B' is inferable from 'A' and 'not-A' – assuming 'A' and 'B' to be atomic propositions – although there is a principle under which 'A or B' is inferable from 'A' and a principle under which 'B' is inferable from 'A or B' and 'not-A'.

The analogy is not to be pressed, however. Thus we cannot imagine that anyone would argue

> A
> Therefore A or B
> But not-A
> Therefore B

unless he had suffered a brainstorm, with the second step being somehow dissociated in his mind from the first. For, of course, if you have asserted the disjunction on the ground of the truth of 'A', you are not then in a position to assert 'B' on the ground of the truth of 'A or B' and 'not-A'. Each step of the argument is valid, but taking the first step invalidates taking the second. We have essentially the same situation in the circular argument

> A
> Therefore A or B
> But not-B
> Therefore A

where now it is the second limb of the disjunction that is denied. We can say in general that it is only possible to use a disjunction in combination with the negation of a disjunct as grounds for asserting the other disjunct if the disjunction is known independently of believing either disjunct.

What is called a principle of inference gives expression to forms under which a proposition Q is inferable from propositions $P_1, \ldots, P_n$, but it does so through giving expression to forms under which the truth of $P_1, \ldots, P_n$ would *serve as a ground* for asserting Q. This is why *If p and if not-p then q* and *If p and if q then p* do not count as principles of inference, despite the fact that any proposition is inferable from contradictory propositions and that a proposition is inferable from any pair of propositions of which it is a member. If *per impossibile* 'A' and 'not-A' were both true, then we should have a ground for asserting their conjunction, but it would be absurd to claim that we should have such a ground because 'A' and 'not-A' are contradictories. And we should allow, in the light of the transitivity principle *If p → q and if q → r then p → r*, that the truth of 'A → B' and 'B → B' could be seen as a ground for asserting 'A → B', but would find unintelligible the claim that the truth of this pair of material conditionals could be seen as a ground for asserting 'A → B' because this proposition was a member of the pair.

So the conclusion of the arguments

>   If A and if B then A and B
>   If A and B then A
>   Therefore if A and if B then A,

>   If A then A or B
>   If A or B and if not-A then B
>   Therefore if A and if not-A then B

are to be regarded as *rogue* hypotheticals, in that their antecedents are introduced as propositions whose truth would serve as a ground for asserting the respective consequents when – assuming that 'A' and 'B' are atomic – there are no forms under which they could do so. Not that this disparity between premisses and conclusion means that the arguments should be regarded as invalid. Defective certainly, but as hypothetical syllogisms they constitute valid arguments, as will become evident when we broach the question of the root form of arguments with a hypothetical premiss or premisses and a hypothetical conclusion.

44. The notion of asserting one proposition on the ground, actual or potential, of the truth of another, can be taken in two ways, according to whether the ground is construed as a ground simpliciter or one that is 'relative to the subject'. Because of the connection between ground and inference – that if the truth of P serves as a ground for asserting Q then Q is inferable from P – it is easy to assume that one can only be justified in asserting one proposition *on*

the ground of the truth of another when the former is inferable from the latter. This assumption, however, cannot be reconciled with the distributive character of the concept of a ground – that if the truth of *P* and *Q* serve as a ground for asserting *R* then the truth of *P* alone serves as a ground for asserting *R* on the ground, actual or potential, of the truth of *Q* – which we have seen to be the condition of an argument's having dialectical variants (*vide* §§25–7).

This is clear from the conclusion of (v), where 'Y' is asserted on the potential ground of the truth of 'not-E', although it is not inferable from it, as also from the conclusion of (vii), where 'Y' is asserted on the actual ground of the truth of 'not-E', although it is not inferable from it. If it is then asked how in that case the truth of the disjunction can possibly afford a ground for asserting 'Y' on the ground of the truth of 'not-E', the answer is that in making the thetical or hypothetical assertion the author is not introducing 'not-E' as a proposition whose truth serves, or would serve, as a ground for asserting 'Y', but *only as a proposition whose truth serves, or would serve, him* as a ground for asserting 'Y'. And this he is in a position to do if he knows the disjunctive premiss of his argument independently of believing either disjunct – as, by so arguing, he gives the hearer to understand that he does (*vide* §13).

A hypothetical in which the ground expressed in the antecedent is thus relative to the speaker, it will be convenient to call *material*. Of course, it is not the case that the ground for asserting such a hypothetical has to consist in the truth of a disjunction or other equivalent truth-functional statement. It may consist in the truth of some general proposition. But where it does, the generality will be accidental as in 'The books on the bottom shelf of my bookcase are all bound in red'. I cannot remember, say, the colour of my copy of the *Tractatus* but I can see at a glance that the books on the bottom shelf are all bound in red, and so I am led to assert that if my copy of the *Tractatus* is on the bottom shelf then it is bound in red. Here the truth of the statement expressing the ground for my assertion simply consists in the truth of a conjunction whose conjuncts ascribe the property of being red to each of the books on the bottom shelf. We call the generality 'accidental' because the statement's truth can be cashed in this way.

45. Now the distinction between the two readings of 'If Russell admires himself then he admires someone who admires himself' – which we drew in §18 to illustrate the dialectical ambiguity of the hypothetical form – is the distinction between the antecedent's being introduced as a proposition whose truth would *serve the speaker* as a ground for asserting the consequent and its being introduced as a proposition whose truth would serve as a ground – a ground simpliciter – for asserting the consequent. Where the latter circumstance holds, there is always the question of the *form or aspect* under which it is so introduced, and in many cases it will be so introduced in virtue of bearing to the consequent a formal relation – a relation which requires for its

expression schematic letters: letters for propositions, names, predicates, relations. This is illustrated by the strong reading of the above hypothetical, where the antecedent is introduced as a proposition whose truth would serve as a ground for asserting the consequent in virtue of bearing to it the formal relation *a has R to itself : a has R to something that has R to itself*. This relation, of course, is none other than that which constitutes the logical form of the deductive argument whose (degenerate) variant has this hypothetical as its conclusion. Here, since the antecedent expresses a logical ground for asserting the consequent, the formal relation is one that finds expression in purely formal terms, but often the formal relation involved in a hypothetical will be *impure*, requiring for its expression actual propositions, names, predicates.

46. If *v* is the hypothetical variant of which a given hypothetical *h* is to be seen as the conclusion – what we called in §20 the variant relevant to *h* – then the formal relation, if any, that is involved in asserting *h* will obviously depend on the form of the argument of which *v* is a variant and which premisses, if any, of the parent argument are retained as premisses of *v*. This means that to determine this relation in a given case we have to operate on the schema that represents the form of the parent argument by removing from it any schematic letters that are exemplified in the premisses (if any) of *v* and replacing them throughout by the expressions – propositions, names, predicates – that exemplify them. If any sub-schemas, however modified, remain after this operation, they will represent the terms of the formal relation involved in asserting *h*.

We illustrate the procedure first by applying it to the hypotheticals in the variants of the disjunctive syllogism, beginning with 'If either E or Y and if not-E then Y'. Since in this case *v* has no premisses, none of the letters in the schema

> Either *p* or *q*
> Not-*p*
> Therefore *q*

suffers replacement by a proposition, and so the relevant formal relation is *either p or q, not-p : q*. That is to say, the hypothetical exemplifies the principle of disjunctive syllogism. If we now apply the procedure to 'If either E or Y then Y', where *v* has 'Not-E' as premiss, the parent schema is transformed into

> Not-E
> Either E or *q*
> Therefore *q*

and so, given the truth of 'Not-E', it follows that the antecedent of this hypothetical would serve as a ground for asserting the consequent in virtue of bearing to it the (impure) formal relation *either E or q : q*, which abstracts from the content of the second disjunct. If, however, we apply the procedure to the hypothetical 'If not-E then Y', where v now has the disjunction as a premiss, both 'p' and 'q' in the parent schema are replaced by propositions, and so no sub-schemas remain. We conclude therefore that this hypothetical is only material.

As a further illustration of the procedure, we take the three hypotheticals relating to Keynes, beginning with 'If Keynes is a Cambridge economist and if Keynes is married to a Russian ballerina then some Cambridge economist is married to a Russian ballerina'. Since v in this case is a degenerate variant, the parent schema

> Fa
> Ga
> Therefore something (that is) F is G

remains intact, but if we apply the procedure to 'If Keynes is married to a Russian ballerina then some Cambridge economist is married to a Russian ballerina', the schema is transformed into

> Keynes is a Cambridge economist
> G (Keynes)
> Therefore G (something that is a Cambridge economist)

since in this case v has the premiss 'Keynes is a Cambridge economist'. So the antecedent of the hypothetical is introduced as expressing a ground for asserting the consequent in virtue of bearing to it the (impure) formal relation G *(Keynes) : G (something that is a Cambridge economist)*, which abstracts from the content of the second predicate. Finally, in the case of 'If Keynes is a Cambridge economist then some Cambridge economist is married to a Russian ballerina', where v has the premiss 'Keynes is married to a Russian ballerina', we obtain the schema

> F (Keynes)
> Keynes is married to a Russian ballerina
> Therefore F (something that is married to a Russian ballerina)

and so here the relevant formal relation is F *(Keynes) : F (something that is married to a Russian ballerina)*, which is again impure.

Where the formal relation in these examples is impure, the speaker will only be in a position to assert the consequent on the potential ground of the truth of the antecedent because he knows a certain proposition to be true, namely that which forms the premiss of the variant relevant to the hypothetical in question. This does not mean, however, that he is wrong to introduce the antecedent as a proposition whose truth would serve as a ground for asserting the consequent, as opposed to one whose truth would serve *him* as such a ground. That Keynes is married to a Russian ballerina *is* a ground for asserting that some Cambridge economist is married to a Russian ballerina, notwithstanding that the ground is only available to one who knows that Keynes is a Cambridge economist. That Eliot did not die before 1940, on the other hand, is no ground for asserting that Yeats died before that date, though it might be *this man's* ground for asserting that he did.

47. The procedure we have outlined is essentially one for determining what formal relation is involved in asserting a given hypothetical, assuming that a formal relation is involved in asserting it. It does not serve, as it stands, to determine whether an arbitrary hypothetical is material or not – whether the ground expressed therein is only relative to the speaker or a ground as such. We can see this from an example suggested by a remark that Wittgenstein makes where he is discussing statements running 'If such and such had been so then . . .'. He mentions a film in which he heard a father tell his daughter that he ought to have married a different woman: referring to this other woman, the father says *'She* ought to have been your mother!'[23] The question then is, What is wrong with the father's implied hypothetical 'If I had married *her*, she would have been your mother'?

Using 'Paul' for the father's name, 'Sarah' for the daughter's and 'Mary' for the name of the woman the father thinks he ought to have married, the parent of the relevant hypothetical variant will be the argument

> Sarah is Paul's daughter
> Paul married Mary
> Therefore Mary is Sarah's mother

taking the second premiss here to imply that Mary is the only woman Paul has had a child by. Now the form under which this argument is valid can be represented by the schema

> a is b's daughter
> b married c
> Therefore c is a's mother

– taking the letters to stand in for beings of the appropriate sex – in which case we are left with the schema

> Sarah is Paul's daughter
> Paul married c
> Therefore c is Sarah's mother

once we remove the schematic letters that are exemplified in 'Sarah is Paul's daughter'. But we are not thereby entitled to infer that the hypothetical 'If Paul married Mary then Mary is Sarah's mother' is not material, with the antecedent being introduced as a ground for asserting the consequent under the respective forms *Paul married c : c is Sarah's mother*. Otherwise it would admit of the wording 'If Paul had married Mary, Mary would have been Sarah's mother', just as 'If Keynes married a Swedish ballerina then some Cambridge economist married a Swedish ballerina' admits of the wording 'If Keynes had married a Swedish ballerina then some Cambridge economist would have married a Swedish ballerina . . . '!

Here we recognise that the hypothetical is material because it is clear that someone is only in a position to advance the argument above, asserting 'Mary is Sarah's mother' on the grounds that Sarah is Paul's daughter and that Paul married Mary if he knows that Sarah is Paul's daughter independently of knowing that she is his daughter by Mary or that she is his daughter by another woman. And so likewise someone is only in a position to assert 'If Paul married Mary then Mary is Sarah's mother' on the ground that Sarah is Paul's daughter if this same condition holds. And now the true state of affairs asserts itself, for if we operate on the schema

> *a* is *b*'s daughter by *c* or someone else
> *b* married *c*
Therefore *c* is *a*'s mother

removing from it the letters that are exemplified in the premiss 'Sarah is Paul's daughter by Mary or someone else', we are left with no sub-schemas to represent a formal relation between the antecedent and consequent of our hypothetical.

A second reason – one pointing in the opposite direction – why this procedure cannot be used to determine whether an arbitrary hypothetical is material or not has been alluded to in §45, where we spoke of the form or aspect under which the antecedent of a hypothetical is introduced when it is introduced as a proposition whose truth would serve as a ground for asserting the consequent. It may indeed be inferred that if no schematic letters are left outstanding in the parent schema when the procedure is carried out, then the hypothetical in question does not involve a formal relation, but this is not to say that it is therefore material. It is true that we are justified in concluding that the hypothetical 'If not-E then Y' is only material, for where the letters in the parent schema are all propositional ones, the antecedent of a hypothetical will only be a proposition whose truth would serve as a ground for asserting the consequent if it bears to it a relation that requires one or more propositional letters for its expression – as, for example, the relation *E or q : q*. Where, however, the parent schema contains name letters, the antecedent of a hypothetical may still express a ground simpliciter for asserting the consequent, even though none of these letters remain when the described procedure is carried out. This is possible in a case where the name letters stand in for demonstrative expressions.

Let us take, as a simple example, the hypothetical statement 'If that creature has lungs then that creature is a lung-fish', where this is asserted on the ground that the creature referred to is a fish. (A lung-fish, one of the so-called Dipnoi, has both lungs and gills.) Here the schema representing the form of the parent argument will be

$$a \text{ is a fish}$$
$$a \text{ has lungs}$$
$$\text{Therefore } a \text{ is a lung-fish}$$

which leaves no sub-schemas outstanding once the name letter is replaced by the expression 'that creature'. We may therefore infer that the antecedent of this hypothetical is not introduced as a proposition whose truth would serve as a ground for asserting the consequent in virtue of any *formal* relation it bears to it. All the same, it is clear from the ground on which the hypothetical itself is asserted that the antecedent and consequent are here viewed *under a certain aspect* and that it is under this aspect that the former is seen as a proposition whose truth would serve as a ground for asserting the latter. The aspect in question is, of course, that of referring to the same *fish*. If we now use a name letter with an attached subscript to symbolise the relation in which these two propositions stand through referring to the same fish, we might draw the following contrast and say that whereas the relation involved in asserting 'If that creature is a fish and if that creature has lungs then that creature is a lung-fish' is the formal relation a *is a fish, a has lungs : a is a lung-fish*, the relation involved in asserting 'If that creature has lungs then that creature is a lung-fish' is the *quasi*-formal relation a_{fish} *has lungs : a_{fish} is a lung-fish*.

48. It is evident that a hypothetical that is not material is one that allows for the concomitant denial of the antecedent or affirmation of the consequent, so that the above hypothetical, for example, admits of the wording 'If that creature were one with lungs, it would be a lung-fish'. For where the antecedent and consequent of a hypothetical enter the statement, not only *in propria persona* – as propositions with such and such truth-values – but under such and such a form or aspect, they make their appearance, so to speak, in a guise that propositions with different truth-values could wear.

In this connection it is important to realise that the *same* antecedent may enter different hypotheticals under different forms. It has, for example, been questioned whether 'any really coherent theory of the contrafactual conditional of ordinary usage' is possible, on the ground that we are at a loss how to adjudicate between such statements as

If Bizet and Verdi had been compatriots, Bizet would have been Italian
If Bizet and Verdi had been compatriots, Verdi would have been French.[24]

The first thing to remark here is that if we are at a loss how to adjudicate between these statements then we are equally at a loss how to adjudicate between 'If Bizet and Verdi were compatriots, Bizet was Italian' and 'If Bizet and Verdi were compatriots, Verdi was French'. No peculiar difficulty attaches to wording the hypothetical in the non-indicative form. But, in any case, it is not that we are at a loss how to adjudicate between the statements, as if they were somehow locked in a competition for our acceptance. There is simply no question of adjudicating between them. We are happy to affirm either hypothetical indifferently. We are happy to affirm the first hypothetical because it is the conclusion (in 'counterfactual' dress) of the hypothetical variant of

> Verdi was Italian
> Bizet and Verdi were compatriots
> Therefore Bizet was Italian

in which the true proposition 'Verdi is Italian' is retained as a premiss, and we are happy to affirm the second because it is the conclusion of the hypothetical variant of

> Bizet was French
> Bizet and Verdi were compatriots
> Therefore Verdi was French

in which the true proposition 'Bizet was French' is retained as a premiss. Being then happy to affirm either indifferently, we may go on to marry the two hypotheticals and infer that if Bizet and Verdi had been compatriots then one would have been Italian and the other French, from which we may infer by *reductio* that they were not compatriots.

If we think that we ought somehow to be able to choose between affirming the one or the other 'counterfactual', or that we ought to be able to do so if a coherent theory of such statements is possible, that is because we fail to appreciate that the common antecedent of the two hypotheticals – which is rendered explicit in the expansion 'If it had been true that Bizet and Verdi were compatriots . . .' – enters the two statements under different forms: it enters the first under the form *a and Verdi were compatriots* and the second under the form *Bizet and a were compatriots*. That the common antecedent of the two statements makes its appearance under different forms is, of course, but another aspect of the dialectical ambiguity to which the hypothetical form of statement is heir, and it could be signalled by emphasising the constant element in the schemas representing the different forms under which the antecedent is introduced. So in the present case we might stress now the one name in the two statements – 'If Bizet and *Verdi* had been compatriots then Bizet would have been Italian' – and now the other – 'If *Bizet* and Verdi had been compatriots then Verdi would have been French'.

Should we side with one who says 'If wishes were horses, beggars would ride' or with one who says 'If wishes were horses, no one would ride'? Counselled by logic, we should make the diplomatic response 'Well, if wishes were *horses*, beggars would ride, but then again if horses were *wishes*, no one would ride'. Here, where the common antecedent is an identity, reversing the order of the terms helps to throw the difference of form into relief.

49. So we are justified in affirming either hypothetical and *in that sense* there is no question of adjudicating between them. But may we not say that there is no question of adjudicating between them because *both are true*? And yet what can it mean to ascribe truth (or falsity) to a hypothetical – a statement whose Mood portrays not the act of asserting a proposition, but that of asserting one proposition on the potential ground of the truth of another?

Here it is natural to point to our practice of predicating 'true' of a hypothetical if we hold the premisses of the relevant variant to be true and the variant valid. The practice, of course, is not to be gainsaid, only it is to be observed that it is modelled on our practice of predicating 'true' of a statement that is simply assertoric if we hold it to be validly inferable from other such truths. Not that this practice affords us with a model in all cases, for there is the obvious proviso that we should normally only be prepared to pronounce a material hypothetical true if, along with the speaker, we held the premisses of the relevant variant true independently of believing the antecedent of the hypothetical to be false or its consequent true. Otherwise we should convey the false impression that the truth of the antecedent would also serve us as a ground for asserting the consequent.

As regards the negative, we are prepared to predicate 'not true' of a hypothetical if it has a true antecedent and a false consequent, because we then know that, however the hypothetical is to be read, there can be no valid variant with true premisses which has as its conclusion a hypothetical with that same antecedent and consequent. Of course, we are prepared to say the same of a hypothetical that is not material, whatever the truth-values of its antecedent and consequent, if we believe that the truth of the former would not serve as a ground for asserting the latter. And we shall hold such a belief if we believe that that there is no valid hypothetical variant with true premisses of which it can be seen as the conclusion.

In these ways we have, via the concept of a hypothetical variant, an analogical footing for predicating 'true' and 'not true' of hypotheticals. But since the clause forming a hypothetical is not a proposition, there is no question of giving the truth-conditions of such a statement: there is no question of giving the conditions under which such a statement is true, as distinct from the conditions under which we are prepared to predicate 'true' of it, or the analogy of our practice in predicating 'true' of a statement that is simply assertoric when it is assertible on inferential grounds. To assume otherwise is simply to deny the complex Mood a statement has as a hypothetical, assimilating it to the Mood of one that is simply assertoric. It may *seem* plausible to claim, for instance, that a hypothetical is true just in case there is a (possibly empty) set of true propositions from which, together with the antecedent(s) of the hypothetical, the consequent is inferable, but to endorse that claim would be to allow that a hypothetical has the same Mood as a statement running 'There is a (possibly empty) set of true propositions from which . . . ' and thus to deny in effect that there is such a concept as that of a hypothetical variant of an argument.

One of the consequences of the assumption that hypotheticals have truth-conditions is the invocation of the machinery of possible worlds – possible worlds in which there are more or less close counterparts to the objects in the actual world – to 'explain the simultaneous truth' of such contrasting hypotheticals as those of §48. Thus in the case of the first hypothetical it is said that we are concerned with the closest possible worlds to ours in which a not-too-close counterpart of Bizet is a compatriot of a close counterpart of Verdi, and in the case of the second with the closest possible worlds to ours in which a not-too-close counterpart of Verdi is a compatriot of a close counterpart of Bizet. Then the first hypothetical is true, since the relevant class of possible worlds are worlds in which a not-too-close counterpart of Bizet is Italian and the second is true, since the relevant class of possible worlds are worlds in which a not-too-close counterpart of Verdi is French.[25]

Here it is clear that the description of the possible worlds relevant to the two hypotheticals is simply a projection into the metaphysical language of 'counterpart theory' of the dialectical difference between them – that their common antecedent makes its appearance under different forms. Where the constant element in the schemas representing the two forms is 'Verdi', the relevant possible worlds contain close counterparts of the composer of that name, with indifferent counterparts of Bizet, and where the constant element is 'Bizet', the relevant possible worlds contain close counterparts of the composer of that name, with indifferent counterparts of Verdi. The projection is wholly illegitimate, being one that distorts a dialectical difference between hypotheticals into a difference of content, albeit one about possible worlds, and the factor causing the distortion is the assumption that hypotheticals have truth-conditions.

50. It is because the clause forming a hypothetical is not a proposition that we are embarrassed to say what the principle of an argument by *modus ponens* is. For it is for this reason that we are not able to formulate a general hypothetical *corresponding to* the argument schema of an argument with a

hypothetical premiss, as we are in the case of a standard argument. So, failing *such* a general hypothetical, *how* are we to express the principle of *modus ponens*? The canonical expression for the principle of an argument is by means of a general hypothetical, so in that case *how* is one to be framed that will give expression to the principle of *modus ponens*? One thing at least is clear: if the principle is one that belongs to logic then it cannot be expressed by a hypothetical that itself alludes to the hypothetical form.

In the light of the concept of a hypothetical variant, it is not hard to see what the answer to our question must be. For if we have resort to the notion of a (possibly empty) set of *true* propositions, we can first formulate the principle by

> If Γ_t: *therefore if P then Q* is a valid argument and if *P* is true then *Q* is true

where the Greek capital with the subscript represents such a possibly empty set and the English capitals are (syntactic) propositional letters. With the next step we avail ourselves of the fact that Γ_t: *therefore if P then Q* is a hypothetical variant of Γ_t, P : *therefore Q*, and so transform this into

> If Γ_t, P : *therefore Q* is a valid argument and if *P* is true then *Q* is true

which in turn gives way to

> If *Q* is inferable from Γ_t, P and if *P* is true then *Q* is true

where the non-logical constant 'if' has disappeared from the body of the principle altogether. We have to remember, however, that the major premiss of an argument by *modus ponens* may be a hypothetical with more than one antecedent, and so we need the following to express the principle of *modus ponens* in its full generality

> If *Q* is inferable from $\Gamma_t, P_1, \ldots, P_n$ and if $P_1, \ldots, P_n$ are true then *Q* is true

or more compendiously

> If *Q* is γ-inferable from $P_1, \ldots, P_n$ and if $P_1, \ldots, P_n$ are true then *Q* is true

where, of course, *Q* is γ-inferable from $P_1, \ldots, P_n$ just in case there is some (possibly empty) set of true propositions from which, together with $P_1, \ldots, P_n$, *Q* is inferable.

In the same way, we arrive at the following

> If *Q* is γ-inferable from *P* and if the contradictory of *Q* is true then the contradictory of *P* is true

as an expression for the principle of *modus tollens*. Here too a more general statement of the principle is possible, which will run

> If Q is γ-inferable from $P_1, \ldots, P_n$ and if the contradictory of Q is true then for some P_i the contradictory of P_i is true, where $1 \leq i \leq n$.

51. But is this not the height of paradox? For having denied in §49 that a hypothetical has truth-conditions – and thus rejected the claim that a hypothetical is true just in case the consequent is γ-inferable from the antecedent(s) – we are now identifying the principle of a *modus ponens* with that of an argument in which the major premiss is just such a statement! So we are in effect identifying the principle of (i) with that of

> The proposition that Yeats was outlived by Eliot is γ-inferable from the proposition that Yeats died before 1940
> Yeats died before 1940
> Therefore Yeats was outlived by Eliot!

If there seems a paradox here, that is because we are overlooking the distinction between argument form and root form. The argument form of (i) is quite distinct from that of the above argument – which we might call the *standard counterpart* of (i) – and so to identify their root forms is in no way to assimilate the one argument to the other. We do not thereby compromise the integrity of (i) as an argument in which the major premiss is a statement with a different Mood from that of the major premiss of its standard counterpart.

In practice, an argument by *modus ponens* displaces its standard counterpart. Outside the study we do not traffic in arguments with premisses asserting that one proposition is inferable from another together with some (possibly empty) set of true propositions. We do not need to. In the present instance it is clear that anyone who is in a position to draw the inference in the counterpart argument, and so use the inferential statement as a premiss from which, together with 'Yeats died before 1940', to infer 'Yeats was outlived by Eliot', must believe that statement independently of believing that the first proposition is false or the second true: he will believe it, say, because he has learnt that Eliot died in 1963. But in that case he will be able to dispense with the cumbersome inferential premiss in favour of the simple hypothetical and so execute a *modus ponens* instead.

52. It appears, then, that the principles of *modus ponens* and *modus tollens* relate not to this or that form of logical inference, but to the logical form of inference as such. They are principles, not of logical inference, but of the logic of inference. When we execute a *modus ponens*, we are giving implicit recognition to that property of inference whereby from a set of propositions that are true only a true proposition is inferable and when we execute a *modus*

tollens, we are giving implicit recognition to that property of inference whereby a set of propositions from which a false proposition is inferable cannot all be true. There is therefore a certain irony in the fact that in the tradition these two principles should be brought under the same hat as the principles of *modus ponendo tollens* and *modus tollendo ponens* (*vide* §1). Arguments by *modus ponens* and *modus tollens* are presented to the beginner in logic, along with examples of disjunctive syllogism, as paradigms of logically valid inference, as indeed they are, but without recognition of the fact that they are on a quite different footing.

It will be remembered that this whole enquiry began with the question of how logic can be the theory of formal inference when the form under which (i) is valid is not a logical form. We were right in thinking that it was not a logical form, because 'the form under which (i) is valid' was there taken to refer to the form represented by its argument schema, and the word 'if', the constant element in the schema, is not a logical constant. But the question whether the form under which an argument is valid is a logical form does not relate to its argument form but to its root form, and so the question is whether logic, as the theory of formal inference, should be taken to encompass the principles of (what we are calling) the logic of inference along with the principles of logical inference. And now it is in a sense immaterial how we answer this question, for even if we answer it in the negative and so conclude that there are formally valid arguments of which logic does not take account, that assertion loses its air of paradox when we learn that the principles of these recalcitrant arguments are principles of the *logic* of inference. In the light of this insight, we can hardly cavil at the claim that an argument by *modus ponens* or *modus tollens*, though on a different footing from an argument of either of the other two classical *modi*, is nevertheless a paradigm of a logically valid argument.

53. Where the argument form of an argument is different from its root form, it needs to be shown that what is alleged to be the principle of the argument *is* the principle of the argument. That is to say, it needs to be shown that the alleged principle serves to explain how an argument with that argument form is valid. This was shown in the case of a hypothetical variant by appealing to the distributive character of the concept of a ground. It will be remembered that we appealed to this in order to show that the principle of disjunctive syllogism serves to explain how an argument that is a dialectical variant of a disjunctive syllogism is valid.

In the case of an argument that has a hypothetical amongst its premises, it is shown by appealing to the condition that has to be satisfied if you are to be justified in asserting a given hypothetical. Thus to show that the alleged principle of a *modus ponens* is the principle of an argument of that form, we simply appeal to the fact that you can only be justified in asserting the major premiss of such an argument if the consequent of the hypothetical is γ-inferable from its antecedent(s). It then follows, by the principle we have elicited, that if you are justified in asserting the major premiss and if the minor premiss(es) are true, then the conclusion is true.

We think of an argument by *modus ponens* as intuitively valid, no less so than a disjunctive syllogism, notwithstanding the fact that there can be no question – a hypothetical being what it is – of seeing that it is impossible for its premisses to be true without the conclusion being true, as we can see that it is impossible for the premisses of a disjunctive syllogism to be true without the conclusion being true. So should we deny that we have such an intuition and conclude that we are somehow deluded in thinking that we can *see* (i) to be valid? Not at all! Only we do not see that it is impossible that the premisses should be true without the conclusion being so. Our intuition of the argument's validity is explained by the implicit recognition of the relation that has to obtain between the antecedents and consequent of a hypothetical if one is to be justified in asserting it.

54. When it comes to formulating the principle of an argument that has a hypothetical conclusion as well as a hypothetical premiss, it is evident that the notion of γ-inferability enters in connection with both conclusion and premiss. Thus to formulate the principle of the incomplete *modus ponens*

> If Carr is out then if Allen is out then Brown is not out
> Carr is out
Therefore if Allen is out then Brown is not out

we need the hypothetical

> If R is γ-inferable from P, Q and if P is true then R is γ-inferable from Q

or to give the more general statement

> If Q is γ-inferable from $P_1, \ldots, P_n$ and if $P_1, \ldots, P_r$ are true then Q is γ-inferable from $P_{r+1}, \ldots, P_n$ where $1 \leq r \leq n$.

So again, as with a *modus ponens*, the argument from Carroll's paradox has the same root form as an argument in which premisses and conclusion are statements that are simply assertoric.

In an incomplete *modus ponens* the conclusion and major premiss are so related that the parent of the variant relevant to the former is the same as the parent of the variant relevant to the latter. It is this which makes it an *incomplete modus ponens*. It is not merely that the inferred hypothetical has the form of a hypothetical, it demands a certain reading (*vide* §20). Thus in the present case, the hypothetical variants relevant to the conclusion and premiss will have the statement 'Someone is always in the shop' as a common premiss.

To show, then, that the principle we have formulated is the principle of an incomplete *modus ponens* is to show that it serves to explain the validity of an argument with a form in which the major premiss and conclusion are so related. To this end we appeal as before to the fact that you can only be justified in asserting a hypothetical if the consequent is γ-inferable from the antecedent(s). It then follows, by the principle we have formulated, that if you are justified in asserting the major premiss of an incomplete *modus ponens* and the minor premiss(es) are true then the consequent of the conclusion is γ-inferable from the antecedent(s). Therefore if you are justified in asserting the major premiss and the minor premiss(es) are true then you are justified in asserting a hypothetical with the antecedent(s) and consequent of the conclusion. Since, however, the variant relevant to the conclusion of an incomplete *modus ponens* has the same parent as the variant relevant to the major premiss, this hypothetical will have the required reading.

If one is without a conception of the argument form of an incomplete *modus ponens* – of how, through the concept of a hypothetical variant, the conclusion of such an argument relates to the major premiss – one might be persuaded, strange as it may seem, that an argument could have the form

> If p then if q then r
>
> p
>
> Therefore if q then r

and yet be invalid! For it is not difficult to construct readings of hypotheticals of these two forms such that one could be justified in asserting the first and its p-antecedent be true without being thereby justified in asserting the second. It has been contended, for example, that we can see that the argument

> If that creature is a fish then if it has lungs then it is a lung-fish
>
> That creature is a fish
>
> Therefore if it has lungs then it is a lung-fish

is invalid by supposing that the creature pointed to is not swimming in fresh water, where lung-fish are normally found, but in the sea, for in that case the creature is likely to be a member of the dolphin family if it has lungs, despite its unusual shape. So does it not follow that one could be justified in asserting the major premiss of the argument and the minor premiss be true, so that the consequent of the conclusion is γ-inferable from its antecedent, without being justified in asserting that if the creature in question has lungs then it is a lung-fish?[26]

The reply to make here is that, yes, it certainly follows that one could be justified in asserting the major premiss and the minor premiss be true without being justified in asserting a hypothetical running 'If that creature has lungs then it is a lung-fish' *in which* the antecedent enters the statement under the aspect $a_{marine\ animal}$ *has lungs*. But what is not possible is that one should be justified in asserting the major premiss and the minor premiss be true without being thereby justified in asserting *the conclusion of the argument*. It is nothing to the point that in the imagined circumstances a ground would be available to the speaker for asserting that if the creature has lungs then it is not a lung-fish but a member of the dolphin family. For the common parent of the variants relevant to the conclusion and premiss – in the latter's case a degenerate variant – is an argument whose principle is expressed by 'If *a* is a fish then if *a* has lungs then *a* is a lung-fish', and so the antecedent of the inferred hypothetical enters the statement under the aspect a_{fish} *has lungs*. Now it goes without saying that any ground there might be for asserting 'If that creature has lungs then it is one of the dolphin family' could not possibly be such that the antecedent entered the hypothetical under that aspect.

So much, then, may serve in respect of arguments that have a hypothetical conclusion as well as a hypothetical premiss or premisses. We descanted in §20 on the argument forms of an argument by contraposition and a hypothetical syllogism and in the light of the foregoing it is easy to see how the principles of such arguments should be formulated and how these principles serve to explain their validity.

55. Since the conjunction that generates a hypothetical is not a logical constant, it might be said that there is no logic of the hypothetical, or better that there is no logic of the hypothetical *as such*. This is shown by the fact that any argument in which a hypothetical statement is inferred from premisses that are simply assertoric is a dialectical variant of a standard argument, so that it enjoys the same principle as the argument of which it is a variant, and by the fact that any argument in which an inference is drawn from premisses that contain a hypothetical has as its principle, not a principle of logical inference, but of the logic of inference, so that it enjoys the same principle as what we have called its standard counterpart.

It might seem strange therefore that logicians, in formalisations of propositional logic, should have sought to represent a hypothetical, which does not contain a logical constant, by a material conditional. But it is one of the ironies of our subject that it follows from the facts that show that there is no logic of the hypothetical as such that any formally valid argument with hypothetical premisses and/or conclusion converts into a logically valid argument under replacement of the hypothetical(s) by the corresponding material conditional(s). If we divide such arguments into those in which a hypothetical is inferred from premisses that are simply assertoric and those in which a hypothetical is inferred from premisses of which at least one is a hypothetical, then this can be brought out briefly and informally as follows.

In the first place, since an argument of the first class is a hypothetical variant, the proposition asserted by the conclusion of the parent argument will be inferable from the proposition(s) asserted by the premiss(es). But now we know that

If Q is inferable from Γ, P then P → Q is inferable from Γ

and so, for example, the hypothetical variant

> Not-(C and A and B)
> C
Therefore if A then not-B

converts into a logically valid argument under replacement of the conclusion by the material conditional 'A → not-B'. There is, however, an exception to be made in the case of the degenerate hypothetical variant. The reason that one cannot say likewise that the variant

Therefore if not-(C and A and B) then if C then if A then not-B

converts into a valid argument under replacement of the conclusion by a material conditional, is that no sense can be attached to

Therefore not-(C and A and B) → (C → (A → not-B)).

For where is the argument of which this formation can be seen as a *degenerate* case? What will its premisses be? It is true, of course, that we may speak of the tautological material conditional as 'provable on no assumptions', as we speak of the conditional 'A → not-B' as provable on the assumptions 'Not-(C and A and B)' and 'C', and in this way we achieve a convenient generality of expression, but to say that something or other is provable on no assumptions is to make a statement, not to advance an argument, degenerate or otherwise.

In the second place, we note that if Q is γ-inferable from $P_1, \ldots, P_n$ then the material conditional $P_1 \to (P_2 \to \ldots \to (P_n \to Q) \ldots)$ is true and, conversely, that if the material conditional is true then Q is γ-inferable from $P_1, \ldots, P_n$. Hence to each principle of the logic of inference there corresponds a logical principle involving the material conditional. Thus corresponding to the principle of *modus ponens* we have

If $P_1 \to (P_2 \to \ldots \to (P_n \to Q) \ldots)$ is true and if $P_1, \ldots, P_n$ are true then so is Q

and corresponding to the principle of incomplete *modus ponens* we have

If $P_1 \rightarrow (P_2 \rightarrow \ldots \rightarrow (P_n \rightarrow Q) \ldots)$ is true and if $P_1, \ldots, P_r$ are true then so is $P_{r+1} \rightarrow (P_{r+2} \rightarrow \ldots \rightarrow (P_n \rightarrow Q) \ldots)$, where $1 \leq r < n$.

So the *modus ponens* with 'If C and if A then not-B' as major premiss converts into

$$C \rightarrow (A \rightarrow \text{not-B})$$
$$C$$
$$A$$

Therefore not-B

and the incomplete *modus ponens* converts into

$$C \rightarrow (A \rightarrow \text{not-B})$$
$$C$$

Therefore $A \rightarrow$ not-B.

56. With these remarks we reach the end of our investigations. It only remains to say that if logicians have hitherto been unable to provide a coherent account of the principles governing hypotheticals in inference, the reason is not that these are somehow possessed of a complex logic that the grammatical form of hypotheticals makes it difficult to discern and articulate. Thus the case of such statements is not to be compared with that of statements of multiple generality, where it took a logician of Frege's stature, with his invention of the notation of quantifiers and variables, to explicate their inferential role. No, here the reason lies in the failure of logicians to recognise the concept of a hypothetical variant of an argument and thus effect the consequent distinction between what we have called the argument form of an argument and the root form thereof. It then appears that there is no difficulty in articulating the principles of formally valid arguments with hypotheticals as premisses or conclusion. If the argument is a hypothetical variant, it has the same principle as its parent. Otherwise it is a principle of the logic of inference.

Part II

Formal relations

Formal relations

I Exposition

We speak not only of the relation of a city to a country of which it is the capital or of a man to a child of whom he is the father, but of the relation of an object to a function of which it is the argument. But whereas the first relation finds expression in sentences that have in common the expression 'capital of' and the second in sentences that have in common the expression 'father of', the function–argument relation finds expression in complex designations such as 'the capital of Holland' and 'Rembrandt's father', which have no expression in common. For this relation is not one that can be *put into words* at all. We might say, echoing *Tractatus* 4.121, that it is not something we can express by means of language, but something which expresses *itself* in language.

Because there is no expression for the function–argument relation, such a relation is quite unlike a relation proper. By a relation proper I mean a relation as it is understood in predicate logic. Not that a relation proper is something for which there always exists an actual sign in the language, as there does for the relation *capital of* or *father of*. For the purpose of the logician a (first-level) relation is expressed in any sentence (of ordinary discourse) that contains two or more singular terms functioning as logical subjects. Still, it is something we express by means of language, as is shown by the fact that if the language contains no sign for it one can always be introduced. Thus we could introduce by definition a sign for the relation between Leeds and London that is expressed in 'Leeds is farther from Paris than it is from London'.

Frege's thesis that a concept is a particular case of a function embodies the fundamental insight that the sense in which we speak of the relation of an object to a concept it falls under is the same as that in which we speak of the relation of an object to a function of which it is the argument. As there is no expression for the latter, so there is none for the former. If therefore we use the locution '*a* falls under the concept *F*' and write 'Gold falls under the concept *malleable*' in place of 'Gold is malleable', we do not express in words a relation that is expressed in the shorter sentence without words. Frege thus betrays his own insight when he allows himself to be persuaded that because 'falls under' is a transitive verb, it stands for a relation.[1] In place of 'the capital of Holland' we could likewise write 'the value of the function *capital of* for the argument Holland'. Suppose someone now thought that the longer designation contained an expression – *viz*. 'the value of the function – for the argument . . .' – for the relation of an object to a function of which it is the argument. Would this not be manifestly absurd?

If the statement 'There is no expression for the relation of an object to a concept it falls under' strikes us as paradoxical, that is because we are confusing it with a statement like 'There is no expression for the relation of one body to another that lies beneath it' – a statement which demonstrates its own falsity. But the first statement is to be construed as one about the 'grammar' of 'relation' as this is used in 'the relation of an object to a concept it falls under'. It is not as if we were saying there is no expression for a relation which we then, absurdly, go on to use an expression for! In saying, 'The relation of an object to a concept it falls under expresses *itself* in language and is not one that we express by means of language', we have not in the same breath expressed the very relation that we are saying cannot be expressed. Even if we say, 'The relation of an object's falling under a concept relates gold and the concept *malleable*', we are still no nearer to (because infinitely far from) putting into words the relation that is expressed alike in 'Gold is malleable' and 'Gold falls under the concept *malleable*'. We have still only constructed yet another sentence in which that relation expresses itself.

Since 'falls under' is not a relational expression, it follows that phrases of the form 'the concept F' are not singular terms. Unlike 'the city of Leeds', which designates a certain city, 'the concept *malleable*' does not designate a certain concept. Hence we cannot regard the verb and accusative of 'Gold falls under the concept *malleable*' as signs in their own right. In combination they form an expression for a concept, but in themselves they are not expressions *for* anything. Frege of course recognised that phrases of the form 'the concept F' are not concept-words, but if you take 'falls under' to be a genuine *Beziehungswort*, as Frege did in *On Concept and Object*, you have in consistency to construe such phrases as singular terms. Frege was thus forced to equivocate: as a singular term a phrase of this form must stand for an object, so by parity with 'the city of Leeds' it should stand for an object that (somehow) represents a concept. – And yet how easy it is to go astray here! For in our sentence there *is* expressed a relation between gold and the concept *malleable*. So what more natural than to assume that 'falls under' is an expression for that relation? And yet the right conception is so close at hand! For if 'the concept *malleable*' is not an expression for a concept, it cannot stand for the second term of the relation of an object's falling under a concept. And so 'falls under' cannot itself be an expression for that relation. We thus reach the conclusion that the relation expressed *in* our sentence is not expressed *by* it.

The concept–object relation is expressed in the sentence with 'falls under', as it is expressed in 'Gold is malleable', because it is the result of completing a sign for a concept with a sign for an object. The first sentence is the result of completing the sign 'ξ falls under the concept *malleable*' and the second is the result of completing the sign 'ξ is malleable'. Now the concept *concept* (of first-level) and the concept *object* are formal concepts (in the sense of the *Tractatus*), so the description 'is the result of completing a sign for a concept with a sign for an object', is a formal description. Hence it comes to the same thing whether we say that the relation of an object's falling under a concept is expressed in a sentence or that the sentence satisfies this formal description. In other words, for this relation to be expressed in a sentence is for the form *Fa* to be expressed in it.

That is why we say that this relation 'expresses itself' in language. For logical form, as the *Tractatus* says, is not something that we express by means of language but something which expresses itself in language. That a sentence of the form *Fa* is of this form is something which *comes out* in the formal inferences in which it is deployed.

Since it is one and the same thing for the concept–object relation to be expressed in a sentence and for the form *Fa* to be expressed in it, it seems appropriate to call this relation a formal relation. If we use '$\varphi(\ )$' to represent the form of a first-level concept and 'ξ' the form of an object, we may represent this relation by the schema '$\varphi(\xi)$'. Then instead of saying that the relation of an object's falling under a concept is expressed in 'Gold is malleable', we may say that the relation $\varphi(\xi)$ is expressed in this sentence. And the grammatical statement 'There is no expression for the relation of an object to a concept it falls under' will then give way to the statement 'There is no expression for the relation $\varphi(\xi)$', the truth of which is *manifest*.

There will clearly be a hierarchy of formal relations corresponding to the formal concepts *concept of first-level, concept of second-level*, and so on. There will be a similar hierarchy corresponding to the formal concepts *relation of first-level, relation of second-level* and so on. Thus co-ordinate with the relation of an object to a concept it falls under is the relation of a (dyadic) relation to the objects it relates, which may be represented by the schema '$\psi(\xi,\zeta)$'. If you take the verb 'relates' in 'The relation *next* to relates the desk to the window' to be a relational expression, you are confusing a formal relation with a relation proper. Bradley is guilty of this confusion when, in his polemic against relations, he argues that if a relation is to relate its terms it must be something to them, and so must be related to them. That is to say, if a relation is to relate its terms, it must itself stand in a relation to them. – It is not that we cannot speak of the relation of a relation's relating its terms, but if someone expresses himself as Bradley does, he is plainly confusing the formal relation with a relation proper. This comes out in the image Bradley uses to summarise his argument: 'The links are united by a link, and this bond of union is a link which also has two ends; and these each require a fresh link to connect them with the old.'[2]

Moving up one step to the next level in the hierarchy of formal relations, we have the relation of a concept to a (second-level) concept it falls within, which is expressed in, for instance, 'There is at least one moon of Jupiter'. To represent this relation we could, after Frege's manner, use the formal schema '$\omega_\beta(\varphi(\beta))$', where '$\omega_\beta((\beta))$' represents the form of a second-level concept. What is meant by 'relation' here is something quite different from what is meant by it in 'the relation of subordination between concepts', where it expresses a relation proper, though one of second-level. It is true that, being of second-level, there is no simple expression for this relation in the sense of a quotable sign such as we have for some first-level relations (e.g,. 'capital of', 'north of'), but it is expressed *by means of* language. The general hypothetical form is one of such means of expression, as when we say, 'If an object is made of gold then it is malleable'. Here the occurrence of the connective 'if . . . then . . .' shows that the relation expressed in the sentence between the concepts *object made of gold* and *malleable* is not a formal one. In representing the relation of subordination we could not use *only* formal letters.

Frege is often at pains in his writings to insist on the difference between the relation of subordination and that of an object's falling under a concept, which he calls 'the relation of subsumption'; and no doubt with good reason. But if we say, 'And he's surely right to insist on the difference, for what, after all, could be greater than the difference between a relation between two concepts and a relation between an object and a concept?', we are making a mistake. To contrast one relation with another in respect of their terms has no meaning unless the relations are otherwise comparable – are either both formal relations or both relations proper. If we want a relation between an object and a concept that we can contrast with the relation of subordination, we may take that expressed by a sentence of the form 'Nothing except *a* is *F*'. Here we *could* say that this relation, being one between an object and a concept, is quite different from the relation of subordination. But the *ground* for such a contrast is lacking as between the relation of subsumption and the relation of subordination.

Of course, it could be argued that the sense of 'relation' which we have in 'the relation of subordination' is not really the same as that which we have in, say, ' the relation *north of*', though we have called both relations proper. And it would indeed be at best misleading to say that a student, on being introduced to predicate logic, comes to *see* that a relation is expressed by 'If an object is made of gold, it is malleable' as it is by 'Leeds is north of London', but a relation between concepts, not objects. But to concede this is by no means to undermine the contrast we are drawing between formal relations and relations proper. It would be sheer nonsense to say that our student comes to *see* that a relation is expressed in 'Gold is malleable' as it is in 'Leeds is north of London', only a relation of an object to a concept, not of an object to an object.

We should notice in this connection that because Frege holds that truth-values – the True and the False – are objects and that a concept is a function from objects to truth-values, he cannot strictly represent the relation of subsumption as a *formal* relation. In the use *we* have been making of Greek letters, '$\varphi(\ )$' in '$\varphi(\xi)$' holds a place open for concept-signs only, so that for us the relation $\varphi(\xi)$ *is* the relation of subsumption. If therefore we had wished to represent the function–argument relation, i.e., the relation of an object as argument to a function from objects to objects, we should have had to use a letter from a different part of the alphabet, say 'λ'. Then we could have said that the relation $\lambda(\xi)$ is expressed in 'the capital of Holland' but not in 'Gold is malleable'. But since Frege conceives a concept itself as a particular case of a function from objects to objects, there is no question of *his* distinguishing two such uses of formal letters. For him $\varphi(\xi)$ represents alike the formal relation that is expressed in the sentence *and* in the complex singular term. To represent the relation of subsumption as such he has therefore to introduce, or invent, a function which maps the True onto the True, the False onto the False, and objects other than the True and the False onto the False. Thus he represents this relation by the schema '$-\varphi(\xi)$', where the horizontal is a sign for this function: if '$\varphi(\ )$' is replaced by a concept sign and 'ξ' by a proper name, the resultant formation will be a name of the True or the False, according as the sentence following the horizontal is true or false, i.e., according as the object named in the sentence falls under the concept signified or not. Otherwise the resultant formation is a name of the False. Now this representation of the relation of subsumption, which belies the fact that it is a formal relation, can be seen as an objection to holding both that truth-values are objects and that a concept (of first-level) is a function from objects to truth-values. For it is only his espousal of this dual thesis which forces Frege to represent what is a formal relation by a schema incorporating a sign with the intended role of a functional constant.

The notion of a formal relation is worth exploring because, amongst other things, it enables us to understand how the general notion of a sign for function, concept, relation is one under which such a sign is, in Frege's metaphor, 'incomplete'. This can be seen as follows. A formal concept is expressed, or expresses itself, in language through the occurrence of a sign for an object falling under it. Here the thought, and the terminology of *an object falling under a formal concept*, is taken from the *Tractatus*. The thought is that which the *Tractatus* expresses by saying that 'a formal concept is already given with an object falling under it' (4.12721), where something falling under, say, the formal concept *concept of first-level* will be a particular first-level concept. So this formal concept is expressed in language through the occurrence of a sign for a first-level concept. But for this formal concept to be expressed in language *is* for the corresponding formal relation – the relation $\varphi(\xi)$ – to be expressed in language. Hence this formal relation is itself expressed in language through the occurrence of a sign for a first-level concept. So what is here understood by a sign for such a concept must contain as it were the form of the ξ-term of the relation φ(ξ), and so must be incomplete in Frege's sense. Clearly a parallel argument could be constructed for any sign of an object falling under a formal concept (of whatever level) involving the concepts *function, concept, relation*.

With a sign for an object falling under the formal concept *object*, however, the case is different. This concept too is expressed in language through the occurrence of a sign for an object falling under it. That is to say, it is expressed in language through the occurrence of a proper name, i.e., a sign for an object in Frege's sense. But here there is no answering formal relation of which we can say that it is one and the same thing for it and the concept *object* to be expressed in language. (Which is not to say that this formal concept can be expressed in language without some formal relation being expressed too.)

To avoid possible confusion, we should point out that although the *Tractatus* speaks of formal relations as well as formal concepts (see 4.122 and 5.242), what *it* calls a formal relation is *not* what we are calling such. For that work a formal relation is an internal relation, though it is not a relation proper, since for the *Tractatus* only external relations are that. With the contrast we are drawing, however, relations proper include internal relations. For instance, a proposition expressing the relation of subordination may be a necessary one and if it is, it will express an internal relation between concepts.

At 4.126 the *Tractatus* refers to 'the confusion between formal concepts and concepts proper' which, it says, 'pervades the whole of the old logic'. It will not therefore be surprising, if the *Tractatus* is right in this, to find confusion in philosophy between formal relations and relations proper. Indeed we have hinted at such confusion in Frege himself, and in the remainder of the paper I go on to consider two theories that display this confusion. One is the theory that properties and relations are universals and the other is the theory that a fact is a complex. This last we shall consider in relation to views expressed in the *Tractatus* concerning the nature of what it calls a *Sachverhalt* (state of affairs).

2 Universals

Since sentences of the form '*a* falls under the concept *F*' do not express relational propositions, it follows, as we said, that phrases of the form 'the concept *F*' are not singular terms. There is therefore an asymmetry between such phrases and expressions of the form 'the object *a*'. An expression of this form is an expression for an object, but a phrase of the form 'the concept *F*' is not an expression for a concept. It is not an expression for anything.

On the theory of universals, according to which expressions for properties and relations are expressions for universals, there is no such asymmetry. The words I use in saying what the predicate of 'This sheet is white' stands for – *viz.* 'the property of being white' – constitute an expression for the property of being white, *alias* the universal whiteness. And when I use 'the relation *north of*' to say what the relational expression in 'Leeds is north of London' stands for, I am using an expression for the relation *north of*: I am mentioning a relational universal. A familiar difficulty then presents itself: how, in that case, can a sentence be formed from a name and a predicate or from two names and a relational expression? For 'This sheet the property of being white' and 'Leeds the relation *north of* London' are not sentences.

The conception of a property or relation as a universal – something which can somehow be present in its entirety in many things (or pairs of things) at the same time – springs from the confusion of a formal relation with a relation proper. For what is this relation of a property's being present in a thing? Is it a formal relation or a relation proper? It seems, on the one hand, that it must be a formal relation, since it is expressed in the non-relational sentence 'This sheet is white'. According to the theory, this sentence expresses a relation between a sheet, which is a particular, and the property of being white, which is a universal. On the other hand, it seems that this relation must be a relation proper. For the words '(is) present in' constitute an expression for it. The relation expressed in 'This sheet is white' is put into words if I say 'The universal whiteness is present in this sheet'.

So the answer to our question is that the universal–particular relation is a fictitious relation which results from conceiving the thing–property relation as if it were a relation proper.

With this confusion there goes a corresponding confusion between a formal concept and a concept proper. Since the thing–property relation is conceived as if it were a relation proper, the formal concept *property* is conceived as if it were a concept proper. So the phrase 'the property of being white' comes to be seen, absurdly, as an expression for an object falling under this formal concept. It is this fictitious object which is the first term of the proposition 'The universal whiteness is present in this sheet'.

The use of the word 'property' to signify a formal concept is a transference from what might be called its material use, which it retains. This double use can easily lead to confusion. At first sight most of us would probably see no difference between the use of the word in 'White is a property of this sheet' and its use in 'To be white is a property of this sheet'. Now it is true that in the second sentence the word 'property' does signify the formal concept *property*. As the the predicative form 'to be white' shows, this sentence is just another way of writing the sentence 'This sheet has the property of being white'. But in the first sentence, where we have the *name* of a colour, the words 'is a property of' constitute a relational expression, with the word 'property' serving as a relative term like 'father'. Instead of this relational expression we could use 'is present in' and write '(The colour) white is present in this sheet'.

A nice illustration of this confusion occurs in the following passage from Waismann's thesis on the *Tractatus*:

I see, say, a red patch in front of me. Now should I say 'Red is a property of the patch'? Or should I say rather 'It is a property of red to be in that place'? What is here property and what, thing? This question is completely idle. The truth is that our customary forms of speech (substantive, adjective) lose their meaning completely once they are applied to the phenomena themselves.[3]

Here the first of the two quoted sentences is plainly wrong: as it stands it does not fit the context. For when spelled out, the question which is declared to be 'completely idle' is, 'Is the patch the thing and being red the property?' So the first sentence should be recast to read 'To be red is a property of the patch', so that the word 'property' signifies the formal concept here as it does in the second sentence. As the sentence is given, however, the word 'property' has its material use.

We can point up the incoherence in the conception of a property as something which can be present in its entirety in many things at the same time by playing on this double use of 'property': on the theory of universals it is as if when a number of things have a property in common, that property is their common property.

It may be remarked in passing that Locke's conception of a substratum or property-less subject of properties betrays the same confusion, the same ambiguity. It is as if he conceived of the properties belonging to a man as amongst his belongings: as a man is distinct from the things that belong to him, so the subject of a proposition is distinct from the properties than can be truly ascribed to it. It is 'something I know not what'. But now it could be replied: a man may lose all his belongings without acquiring anything in return, but if he loses the property of having belongings, he thereby acquires the property of being destitute.

3 Fact and complex in the *Tractatus*

As we indicated, what formal relation (or relations) are expressed in a sentence will depend on the form (or forms) of that sentence. Now for the *Tractatus* the seat of logical form is not to be found in the subject-predicate and relational sentences of our language, but in what are called 'elementary sentences', of which our ordinary sentences are held to be truth-functions. Since elementary sentences do not contain proper names, i.e. signs for objects in Frege's sense, we cannot strictly use the vocabulary of predicate logic and say that such forms as 'Fa' and 'Fab' are expressed in them. Still, logical forms and hence formal relations will be expressed in them. What particular formal relation is expressed in a given elementary sentence will depend on the form of the objects named in the sentence, and at 2.051 space, time and colour are picked out as (presumably) *some* amongst the forms that simple objects have. Now it is of the greatest importance for an understanding of the *Tractatus* to realise that there are formal relations which involve *only* simple objects. If we object, 'But how can there be *formal* relations *all* of whose terms are simple objects?', we are simply thinking of the objects of the *Tractatus* on the analogy of what Frege calls objects. This is not to say that there can be no relations proper between simple objects at all. If '*ABC*' is a specimen elementary proposition – assuming that there can be one containing only three names – we can regard it as expressing a relation proper between any two of the objects named in it, just as we can regard 'Leeds is north of London' as expressing a relation between Leeds and London, or a relation (of unequal-level) between the relation and one of the towns. But it is clearly the intention of the *Tractatus* that the different forms of simple objects should give rise to formal relations, so that a formal relation will be expressed in '*ABC*' whose terms are *A*, *B* and *C*, as a formal relation is expressed in 'Leeds is north of London' whose terms are Leeds, the relation *north of* and London. In which case, of course, we can no more regard the first sentence as logically of the triadic relational form that we can the second.

That this is the intention of the *Tractatus* is clear from a number of remarks, of which I shall instance two. First, we are told at 2. 021 that 'objects make up the substance of the world'. Since substance is defined as form and content (2.025), this can only mean that the form and content of an elementary sentence is determined by the names contained in it: once these are known, the form and content of the sentence is known. (If the remark is thought to allow that the content of an elementary sentence may depend on the order of the names, this is a complication we can ignore.) So it must be possible completely to describe the sentence '*ABC*' by saying that there is expressed in it a relation of the objects *A*, *B*, *C*, as it is possible completely to describe the sentence, 'Gold is malleable' by saying that there is expressed in it a relation of gold and the concept *malleable*. We are able so to describe this sentence only because there is a formal relation of an object to a concept. Therefore, if the form of the elementary sentence can be described likewise, there must be a formal relation having as terms simple objects of the forms of *A*, *B* and *C*.

Second, we learn from 4.221 that elementary sentences consist of names 'in immediate combination'. This clearly means that we are not to suppose that names of simple objects will not hold together 'without a link', so that an elementary sentence has to contain, besides names, an expression which completes them into a sentence. In an elementary sentence the names are in immediate combination in the sense in which this could be said of the three expressions in 'Leeds is north of London'. If we were asked why the three expressions in this sentence are in *immediate* combination, we should reply 'Because one is an expression for a relation and the other two are proper names'. But why is this an answer? Clearly because a sentence containing *only* two names and an expression for a relation cannot assert a relation proper between a relation and two objects, as does, for example, 'Only Leeds is north of London', where the names and the relational expression are not in immediate combination. (*Cf.* 'Leeds alone is north of London'.) So by parity we must conclude that '*ABC*' does not assert a relation proper between three simple objects. But there *is* expressed in the sentence a relation between *A*, *B* and *C*. This relation must therefore be a formal one.

It is true, of course, that we have no idea how an answer to the question why the names in an elementary sentence are in immediate combination would run, and this is presumably why 4.221 goes on to say that 'the question then arises how names do combine to form sentences'. This question arises because although we know *a priori* that names of simple objects do so combine, we cannot apply our usual categories to them, distinguishing some as proper names and others as predicates or relational expressions. If we may go by Waismann's notes, this is what lies behind the metaphor at 2.03: 'In a state of affairs the objects hang in one another like the links of a chain.' The implication is that we could *not* say that in the fact that Leeds is north of London two cities and a relation hang in one another like the links of a chain. Here there would be only one link so to speak – the relation.[4]

But this very metaphor reveals at the same time that the *Tractatus* confuses a formal relation with a relation proper. We are to suppose, on the one hand, that the relation expressed in '*ABC*' between the objects named therein – the relation of their hanging in one another – is a formal relation. But we are told, on the other hand, that *in* the fact 'described' by the sentence the objects hang in one another like the links of a chain. The fact that *ABC* is thus conceived as a *complex* whose constituents are *A*, *B* and *C*. (It is 'a combination of objects' – 2.01.) But this requires that the relation of hanging in one another (of combining with one another) be a relation proper. The fact-complex exists or obtains if the objects are so related; otherwise not.

In the same way, if you say, 'In the fact that Leeds is north of London the relation *north of* relates Leeds to London', you are treating the fact expressed by the relational sentence as if it were a complex consisting of a relation and two cities. And that means that you are treating the relation $\psi(\xi,\zeta)$ as if it were a relation proper. Indeed, we can only read the quoted words as a statement at all because they mimic a formation like 'In this chain this link connects this link to that link'. It is this which creates the illusion that they mean something. But since 'The relation *north of* relates Leeds to London' can only mean 'Leeds is north of London', they translate out as 'In the fact that Leeds is north of London Leeds is north of London', which is pure gibberish.

It is not therefore surprising that Wittgenstein should have come later to think that the *Tractatus* was gravely confused over the issue of fact and complex. In an essay written in 1931, where he clearly has the *Tractatus* in mind, he says that 'a complex is not like a fact' and takes issue with the view that 'the fact that this circle is red (that I am tired) is a complex whose component parts are a circle and redness (myself and tiredness)'.[5] Of course, the *Tractatus* would not count the fact that I am tired as a *Sachverhalt*, but the mistake is the same whether you regard the fact that I am tired as a complex composed of myself and tiredness or the fact that *ABC* as a complex composed of the objects *A*, *B* and *C*. In either case you confound a formal relation with a relation proper.

Part III

Universals: logic and metaphor

Universals: logic and metaphor

No doubt what goes under the name of 'the problem of universals' is a complex of difficulties and in this essay I shall, so far as this is possible, address myself to just one of these: namely, that of our understanding of propositions of the form '*a* has the property *F*' and 'The relation *R* relates *a* to *b*'. It is perhaps natural to assume that such propositions are relational ones and this is indeed the assumption made by those who defend universals. Or more precisely: one of the ways in which the conception of properties and relations as universals finds expression is that propositions of these two forms get deployed as if the verbs they contain were expressions for relations.

On the face of it, a sentence like 'This sheet has the property (quality) of being white' is a mere circumlocution for 'This sheet is white', but when Russell writes: 'If we believe that there is such a universal as whiteness, we shall say that things are white because they have the quality of whiteness',[1] it is plain that he is not wishing to say that if we believe there is such a universal as whiteness, we shall say that things are white because they are white. As the word 'because' indicates, we are to read 'things are white because they have the quality of whiteness' as we should read a sentence like 'This drink is intoxicating because it contains alcohol', in which the verb of the because-clause is undoubtedly an expression for a relation. Not that Russell would go so far as to deny that 'This sheet has the quality of whiteness' expresses the same fact as 'This sheet is white'. The presumption is rather that for one who believes that qualities are universals, the first sentence will give a perspective on the fact expressed which the second does not.

Likewise the sentence 'The relation *north of* relates Edinburgh to London' seems *just* a roundabout way of saying that Edinburgh is north of London, but when Russell writes, 'There is no place or time where we can find the relation "north of"; it does not exist in Edinburgh any more than in London, for it relates the two and is neutral as between them',[2] he cannot mean us to take the clause 'it relates the two' here as doing duty for the sentence 'Edinburgh is north of London', so that in reading this passage we may substitute *sotto voce* this sentence for the clause. If we apply our usual understanding and translate out the clause 'it relates the two', so that we have 'The relation *north of* does not exist in Edinburgh any more than in London, for Edinburgh is north of London and the relation is neutral as between them', the second part of the sentence is oddly out of place and no longer even *seems* to express an intelligible reason for asserting that the relation *north of* does not exist in either of the cities it relates. For what, we should be inclined to ask, can Edinburgh's being north of London have to do with the fact that the relation *north of* does not exist in either Edinburgh or London? Here as before the context requires that we read 'it relates the two' as if the verb were a relational expression like the verb in 'This rod connects the two levers'.

We find this same deployment of the construction 'The relation *R* relates *a* to *b*' in one of Bradley's arguments against the reality of relations, when he infers that if a relation is to relate its terms, it must be something to them, and so must be related to them, which leads, he thinks, to an infinite regress; for then, if the relation is to be related to its terms, there must be further relations between the original relation and the terms it relates, and so on. Here again, we can hardly present the inference 'If the relation *north of* is to relate Edinburgh to London, it must be related to them' in the words 'If Edinburgh is to be north of London, the relation *north of* must be related to them'. The consequent of the second conditional seems oddly out of keeping with its antecedent, which we expect to be followed by a clause like 'London must be south of Edinburgh'. The whole structure of Bradley's dialectic depends upon, and exploits, the apparent relational form of the construction 'The relation *R* relates . . .', as is evident from the image he uses to summarise his argument: 'the links are united by a link, and this bond of union is a link which also has two ends; and those each require a fresh link to connect them with the old.'[3]

The natural reaction to this strange argument is expressed, interestingly enough, by Russell himself in a book written thirteen years after *The Problems of Philosophy*. As he puts it, 'Bradley conceives a relation as something just as substantial as its terms, and not radically different in kind'. He points out that the analogy with chains 'should make us suspicious, since it clearly proves, if it is valid, that chains are impossible, and yet, as a fact, they exist'. And he then goes on: 'There is not a word in his argument that would not apply to physical chains. The successive links are united not by another link, but by a spatial relation.'[4]

But natural though this reaction is, it does nothing to remove the perplexity to which Bradley's dialectic can give rise. And it is clear why. For Russell engages with Bradley on the latter's own terms, so that we have here too – as in 'The successive links are united not by another link, but by a spatial relation' – the same deployment of 'The relation *R* relates (unites) . . .' that we found in his earlier writings. Consequently, all we are left with are opposing contentions, with Bradley claiming that for a relation to relate its terms it must be related to them, and Russell in effect denying this, on the ground that a relation is not something substantial like its terms. For him it is as if the peculiar unsubstantial being of a relation enables it to do what a physical link cannot do: unite two links of a chain without being related to them.

The dizzying feeling that we cannot find our feet in the controversy between Russell and Bradley – that we are at the mercy of language, so that it now seems correct to say one thing, now the other, with no apparent way of deciding which is right – is an expression of our perplexity to know what is going on in language when we use it to reflect on itself, and form sentences that purport to describe the logical structure of propositions which we use in speaking 'about the world'. For the constructions whose deployment in these passages we find so bewildering exploit locutions that we use in such reflections upon language. Thus we way that in 'This sheet is white' there is expressed the relation of a thing's having a property and that in 'Edinburgh is north of London' there is expressed the relation of a relation's relating one thing to another, and in saying these things we are commenting on the logical form of these propositions. But now these 'relations' which we say are expressed in the subject-predicate and relational proposition, *what* are they? Do we put them into words when we say 'This sheet *HAS* the property of being white' and 'The relation *north of RELATES* Edinburgh to London', so that what is expressed in the shorter sentences through their being of the forms '*Fa*' and '*Rab*' achieves verbal expression in the longer sentences? So much at any rate is clear: in their way of handling the constructions '*a* has the property *F*' and 'The relation *R* relates *a* to *b*' Russell and Bradley speak as if this were indeed the case.

As Frege was perhaps the first clearly to recognise, the sign for a property or relation, as opposed to the sign for the subject of a property or the term of a relation, is not a quotable sign: it is not an isolable piece of language. Of course, it is not incorrect to call '(is) white' a predicative expression or 'north of' a relational expression, but what is here being called a predicative or relational expression is logically peripheral to what we should call the sign proper for a property or relation. For the sign that is proper to a property must, of course, have a different form from that which is proper to a relation. We give expression to this difference when we say 'It is of the essence of a property to be *of* something' and 'It is of the essence of a (dyadic) relation to be *between* one thing and another'. What these propositions convey could be expressed at the level of language by saying 'The sign for a property contains the form of a sign for a possible subject of the property' and 'The sign for a relation contains the form of signs for possible terms of the relation'. These formulations are not Frege's, but they express what he meant by calling such signs 'incomplete', as opposed to those signs whose form is such that they do not contain the form of other signs, which he calls 'complete'. Of course, if there are signs containing the form of other signs, as the distinction between signs for properties and for relations requires, then there must be complete signs – otherwise the notion of one sign's containing the form of another would be viciously circular – and amongst these will be signs for the possible subjects of the property of being white and for possible terms of the relation 'north of'; for it seems clear that such signs do not in turn contain the form of yet further signs. And now we can say: the sign (proper) for a property or relation is not a quotable sign because it contains the form of other signs. Instead therefore of speaking of 'the property of being white' and 'the relation *north of*', we might speak of 'the property ξ *is white*' and 'the relation ξ *is north of* ζ', where the letters 'ξ' and 'ζ' serve to show that the sign for a property or relation contains the form of signs for a possible subject or subjects of the property or relation. It then appears that the actual expressions '(is) white' and '(is) north of' are only features of these signs: they might be called 'indices' of these signs, because they indicate to us what particular property or relation is expressed in a sentence.

On the other hand, we should note (as against Frege) that it is wrong to regard common nouns, such as 'city' and 'sheet', in this way. If we use the word 'concept' and call these words 'signs for concepts' (in the sense of 'signs for kinds of thing'), then there is no justification for speaking of 'the concept ξ *is a city*', as there is for speaking of 'the property ζ *is populous*'. This comes out in the fact that a common noun, like a proper name, may flank the 'is' of identity – e.g. 'A cube is (identical with) a solid all of whose faces are squares' and 'A class is not (the same as) a collection'. Then again there are statements like 'A horse is a kind (species) of quadruped', in which 'horse' does not occur predicatively. Thus you cannot infer from this statement that if that animal over there is a horse then it is a kind of quadruped.

So instead of saying that a proposition contains a sign for a property we could say that it contains a sign of the form '$\varphi(\xi)$' and instead of saying that it contains a sign for a relation we could say that it contains a sign of the form '$\psi(\xi,\zeta)$'. But now *as* a sign of the form '$\varphi(\xi)$' we may say that the sign for a property is *at the same time* a sign for (the relation of) a thing's having a property, and *as* a sign of the form '$\psi(\xi,\zeta)$' we may say that the sign for a relation is *at the same time* a sign for (the relation of) a relation's relating one thing to another. (This does not mean, of course, that a proposition containing a sign for a property or relation has also to contain a sign for a particular thing, or two such signs. It may, for instance, be a general proposition containing words like 'something' or 'everything'.) By contrast, the sign for a kind of thing, such as a horse is, is *not* at the same time a sign for a thing's being of that kind.

Now however natural it may seem to use the word 'relation' in this connection, it is of the greatest importance to realise that the use we are making of it is a figurative one: the expressions 'the *relation* of a thing's having a property' and 'the *relation* of a relation's relating one thing to another' are figures of speech. The basis for the implied comparison with a relation proper is clear. In that 'Edinburgh is north of London' is a simple (atomic) proposition containing the names of two cities it expresses a relation between the cities named, and this provides the ground for saying that in 'This sheet is white' there is a relation expressed between a thing and a property, for here we have a simple proposition containing a sign for a thing and a sign for a property. Again, in that 'This rod connects this lever to that one' is a simple proposition mentioning a rod and two levers it expresses a relation between these three things, and this provides the ground for saying that in 'Edinburgh is north of London' there is expressed a relation between a relation and two cities, for here we have a simple proposition containing a sign for a relation and the names of two cities. But that we are speaking figuratively in speaking of 'the thing–property relation' and 'the relation–term relation' is shown by the following: since the sign 'ξ is white', which is a sign for the property of being white, is at the same time a sign for the relation of a thing's having that property, there is no expression in language for the relation of a thing's having a property! And likewise since the sign 'ξ is north of ζ', which is a sign for the relation *north of*, is at the same time a sign for the relation of that relation's relating one thing to another, there is no expression in language for the relation of a relation's relating one thing to another! Admittedly, it sounds paradoxical to say these things, but their truth comes home to us if we say instead, 'There is no expression in language for the relation $\varphi(\xi)$' and 'There is no expression in language for the relation $\psi(\xi,\zeta)$'. Whereas it would, of course, be self-refuting to say that there is no expression in language for the relation ξ *is north of* ζ – or, for that matter, for the relation between concepts that is expressed in a sentence of the form 'Whatever is a so and so is a such and such'. It would therefore be a gross confusion to think that the verb of 'This sheet has the property of being white' gives expression to the thing–property relation expressed in 'This sheet is white', or that 'The relation *north of* relates Edinburgh to London' gives expression to the relation–term relation expressed in 'Edinburgh is north of London'. It is, I believe, this confusion which underlies the conception of properties and relations as universals. But of this more hereafter.

So, to allude to a striking passage at *Tractatus* 4.12, these formal relations, as we may call them, are amongst the things 'which express themselves in language', but which 'we cannot express *by means of* language'. (We call them formal because they are represented by schemas that contain only formal letters, with no admixture of language. Or to put it another way: we call them formal because for either to be expressed in an atomic proposition *is* for that proposition to be of the form '*Fa*' or '*Rab*' as the case may be.) They express themselves in language through the use of signs for (particular) properties and relations: the thing–property relation expresses itself in 'This sheet is white' through the use of a sign for the property of being white and the relation–term relation expresses itself in 'Edinburgh is north of London' through the use of a sign for the relation *north of*. Once again, what we are contending for stands out clearly if we say instead: the relation $\varphi(\xi)$ expresses itself in the first sentence through the use of a sign for the property ξ *is white* and the relation $\varphi(\xi,\zeta)$ expresses itself in the second sentence through the use of a sign for the relation ξ *is north of* ζ.

But now if the sign for a property is at the same time a sign for the relation of a thing's having that property, then it comes to the same thing whether we say that the concept *property* is expressed in a given proposition or the relation of a thing's having a property. And it comes likewise to the same thing whether we say that the concept (dyadic) *relation* is expressed in a given proposition or the relation of a relation's relating one thing to another. So there will be no expression in language for the formal concepts *property* and *relation*, as the *Tractatus* calls them, but they too will 'express *themselves* in language' through the use of signs for (particular) properties and relations. And indeed if we thought that the formal concept *property* could be expressed by means of language, so that in 'This sheet has the property of being white' we had a word for this concept as we do have a word for the (material) concept *property* in 'This man owns the property on the corner', then we should have to say, after all, that the first sentence does put into words the relation of a thing's having a property. And then how could this relation be expressed in 'This sheet is white'? How could it express itself in language any more than the relation a man has to the things he owns?

So we are faced with the question how we are to read sentences containing the words 'property' and 'relation'. These words are common nouns like 'river' and 'horse' and as such enjoy like grammatical rules: they occupy, one might say, the same grammatical space as *kind* words proper, and this is indeed why we use the word 'concept' in connection with them and speak of the concept *property* and the concept *relation*, as we speak of the concept *horse* or the concept *river*. However, it now appears that just as there is no expression in language for the thing–property relation or the relation–term relation, so there is none for the concept *property* or the concept *relation*. When therefore we employ the constructions '*a* has the property F' and 'The relation R relates *a* to *b*' we do not use words expressing these formal concepts, any more than we give verbal expression to the corresponding formal relations.

Frege came to think it a defect in language that it should contain words like 'property' and 'relation', holding that their employment leads inevitably to paradox. If a proposition contains mention of a river or horse, then no difficulty attaches, of course, to saying which river or horse it contains mention of: we do so by using the name of a river or horse such as 'the river Thames' or 'the horse Bucephalus'. But how shall we say which property or relation is expressed in a given proposition? It appears that we can only do so by using expressions like 'the property of being white' and 'the relation *north of*', but we are here confronted with the difficulty that such expressions, not being 'incomplete signs', are not (indices of) signs for properties or relations! (Thus you cannot build a proposition out of 'Edinburgh', 'the relation *north of*' and 'London'.) Being constructed after the pattern of 'the river Thames' and 'the horse Bucephalus', they designate objects – possible subjects of propositions – if indeed they designate anything at all. We are thus, it seems, in the strange position of being hamstrung by language: our means of expression necessarily misrepresent what we mean to express. As Frege puts it:

> Language brands a property as an object, since the only way it can fit the designation of a property into its grammatical structure is as a proper name. But in doing so, strictly speaking if falsifies matters. In the same way, the word 'property' itself is, taken strictly, already defective, since the phrase 'is a property' requires a proper name as grammatical subject; and so, strictly speaking, it requires something contradictory, since no proper name can designate a property; or perhaps better still, something nonsensical.[5]

(Here we need to remember that Frege applies the term 'proper name' to singular terms in general.)

Here, it seems to me, Frege shows that he thinks of our logical discourse, as when we reflect on the form of a proposition by saying that it contains the sign of a property or relation, as vainly trying to express the inexpressible. This comes out in the fact that he takes the phrase 'is a property' as requiring a singular term as logical subject; for this shows that he assumes that in using the word 'property' we are seeking to give expression to a concept: we are seeking to do what, in the case of the word 'river', we have no difficulty in doing. He then infers that because a singular term cannot designate a property, we cannot accomplish what we intend and so he declares the word 'property' to be defective. Thus as he represents the matter, we aim to give expression in language to the formal concept *property*, but we necessarily fail to do so because the word we use for this purpose is confined to the same humdrum grammatical role as 'river' and 'horse'.

Now Frege is right to say that 'the property of being white' is not a predicative sign, not a sign for a property, but the inference to be drawn from this is not, as he thinks, that the word 'property' is somehow defective, being grammatically unsuited to the work we require it to do, but that we do not require this work of it. Indeed, how could we? How could we go so far as to *try* to put into words what expresses itself in language through the use of a sign for a property? If it seems to us that our means of expression necessarily misrepresent what we mean to express by them, then it is an illusion that there is anything that we mean to express by them.

So where are we? We are, of course, grammatically constrained to read the nouns 'property' and 'relation' as if they were expressions for concepts, and yet we say at the same time that there is no expression in language for the formal concepts *property* and *relation* – that these concepts cannot be expressed by means of language! How is that possible? It is possible, I believe, because we resort to a fiction. We read these words as if they were expressions for concepts *representing* those formal concepts. Thus in 'This proposition contains a sign for a property' we read (as we must) the word 'property' as if it gave expression to a concept as it does in 'This name (of a house) is a name of a property of his', but we do not read it as if it gave expression to a concept *tout court*: we read it as if it gave expression to a concept representing the formal concept *property*. There is thus in our logical discourse an element of make-believe: we make believe there are concepts representing formal concepts. The employment of this fiction has to be reckoned amongst the conventions of our language.

In the same way, we are grammatically constrained to read the verbs in 'This sheet has the property of being white' and 'The relation *north of* relates Edinburgh to London' as if they were expressions (indices of signs) for relations, but we read them as if they were expressions for relations *representing* the thing–property and relation–term relations. And, correspondingly, we read the pseudo-singular terms 'the property of being white' and 'the relation *north of*' as if they stood for things or objects representing a certain property and a certain relation. Here again, we have no resort but to read 'the property of being white' as if it were like 'the property on the High Street' in standing for something falling under a concept (proper) – what Frege calls an object – but we read it as if it stood for an object representing the property expressed in 'This sheet is white'. So here we are indulging in a double pretence – that there are relations representing formal relations, and that there are objects representing particular properties and relations.

It is, so it seems to me, by such stratagems of make-believe, that we reconcile the requirements of grammar with the impossibility of expressing by means of language what expresses itself in language.

The upshot then is that the constructions '*a* has the property *F*' and 'The relation *R* relates *a* to *b*' are not relational constructions, though we are constrained to read them as if they were. We read them, however, not as constructions which give expression to the thing–property and the relation–term relation, for no construction can do that, but we employ a fiction and read them as constructions which give expression to relations representing those formal relations. As we remarked, however, Russell and Bradley handle these constructions as if language was here being used to put these formal relations into words. So they are guilty of confusing formal relations, or formal concepts, with relations and concepts proper.

It is true, as we saw, that Russell professes disagreement with Bradley, taking him to task for conceiving a relation 'as something just as substantial as its terms, and not radically different in kind'. But this very criticism, attractive though it seems, implicates Russell in Bradley's own confusion. For why does Russell object to Bradley in this way, representing him as if he had misconceived *what* relations *are*? The answer is surely this: it is because Russell shares with Bradley the assumption that the word 'relation' is an *expression for* a concept, just as the word 'link' is. For it is only if we make this assumption that the nature or constitution of relations can so much as become a question for us. It is only if there is a concept X that there can be a question concerning the nature or constitution of Xs. Once this assumption is made, we shall then naturally wish to contrast the concept allegedly expressed by the word 'relation' with such concepts as *link*, *city*, *triangle* and so on, since it will seem evident that the former concept is of a different kind from any concept under which the term of a relation can fall. For how otherwise could a proposition be formed, for instance, from a relation-sign and the names of two cities? So we have the concept, as we think, and can enquire after the nature of the things (entities) which fall under it, but now all that we can say to characterise them is what we can read off from the attenuated description of the concept – that, as Russell says, they are radically different in kind from anything that can be a term! It is in this way that the picture of relations as immaterial or unsubstantial entities arises.

Strange as it may seem, there is nothing absurd in the idea that the word 'link' should have been used in place of the word 'relation', so that we described the proposition 'Edinburgh is north of London' as containing a sign for a link and formed the sentence 'The link *north of* connects (unites) Edinburgh to London'. If, however, we say 'But in that case we should be giving the word "link" a metaphorical use', we are making essentially the same mistake that Russell makes in his attack on Bradley. For when Russell complains that Bradley conceives a relation as something just as substantial as its terms he is complaining in effect that Bradley takes the verb in 'The relation R connects . . .' to have the literal meaning it has in 'This link connects . . .'. Hence the argument that in order for a relation to unite its terms it must be related to them.

So the verb in this construction has a metaphorical sense – but in that case how do I understand the construction at all? How do I make the transition from my understanding of 'This link connects . . .' to 'This relation connects . . .'? How does my understanding of the former give me *any* purchase on the latter? – But surely we don't want to say that a relation is a material link between its terms! – But then do we wish to say that it is an immaterial one, so that, as Russell would have it, it (mysteriously) connects them without being related to them? Really, this appeal to a metaphorical use of language rests upon the assumption that I can, after all, put into words the relation of a relation's relating one thing to another. For it is only on that assumption that the question whether the verb in our construction is to be understood literally or not can arise.

We must not be misled by the expression 'formal concept' into thinking that a formal concept is a kind of concept as a formal garden is a kind of garden. The concept *property* or *relation* is no more a kind of concept than a clothes horse is a kind of horse. We need always to bear in mind that both the use of the word 'concept' in 'the concept *relation*' and the use of the word 'relation' in 'the relation of a relation's relating one thing to another' are figurative ones. (So that if logicians had used 'the concept *link*' in place of 'the concept *relation*' it would have been the word 'concept', not the word 'link', that was being used figuratively.) That is why we do not even begin to understand Bradley's comparison between this relation and the relation of a link's connecting one link to another, despite the fact that we may struggle to put this or that construction on it. We understand someone who says 'John's affection for her formed a bond between them' because 'He has a great affection for her' and 'He is (physically) bound to her' are both (dyadic) relational propositions, but we are at a loss to understand Bradley's comparison because the foundation for such an understanding is lacking. For in 'The relation *north of* relates . . .' we neither have an expression for a concept, as we do in 'This link connects . . .', nor is the verb an expression for a relation.

I want then to say that the conception of a property or relation as a universal – as something which is present in its entirety, and the same, in the various things (pairs of things) that have it – springs from the confusion of a formal relation with a relation proper. For what is this relation of a property's being *present in* a thing? Is it a formal relation or a relation proper? It seems, on the one hand, that it must be a formal relation, since it is expressed in the non-relational proposition 'This sheet is white'. According to the theory, the form of this proposition is such that this relation is expressed in it. On the other hand, it seems that this relation between a thing and a property must be a relation proper. For the words 'is present in' constitute an expression for it. On the theory of universals, the relation expressed in the proposition is put into words if I say 'The universal whiteness is present in (the particular) this sheet'. Thus with the concept *property* now being conceived as a concept proper, we have in 'the universal whiteness' an expression which purports to stand for something falling under this concept. So we arrive at what is the hallmark of a universal: that whilst it can be predicated of particulars, it can usurp the role of a particular and have things predicated of it.

Thus we might say that on the theory of universals it is as if when a number of things have a property in common, that property is their common property. That is the view which takes possession of us once the thing–property relation is assimilated to a relation proper, so that the logician, no less than the lawyer, is giving expression to a concept in using the word 'property'. And now the property of being red inevitably assumes the guise of being something immaterial – as if it were an etherialised form of the colour red – the colour, so to speak, in abstraction from its various shades. The actual colour, we might say, is not the same in all the things it exemplifies. In that this pillar box and this cherry are both red, the same colour, namely red, is in them both, but it is not the same in both of them because they are of different shades of red. With the universal redness, however, things are different. For are we not speaking unambiguously when we say, pointing to both the pillar box and the cherry, 'This is red'? It is not as if there were different shades to the sense of the predicate 'is red', as there are different shades to the colour.

Nor is it as if the sense of the word were divided up when applied now to this thing, now to that. So is not the property predicated present in its entirety in the things that have it?

In this connection we may be reminded of a passage from the beginning of the *Meno*, where Socrates takes Meno to task for thinking that virtue in a man is different from virtue in a woman. He asks whether Meno thinks that this applies only to virtue and goes on: 'Is it the same with health and size and strength, or has health the same character everywhere, if it is health, whether it be in a man or in any other creature?' And then when Meno agrees that health is the same in a man or a woman, he says:

> And what about size and strength? If a woman is strong, will it be the same thing, the same strength, that makes her strong? My meaning is that in its character as strength, it is no different, whether it be in a man or in a woman.[6]

Here we are inclined to ask what we should be agreeing to if we agreed that strength were the same in a man or a woman. And if we are to take sides on the matter, why should we not say that it is *not* the same in man and woman? For to be a strong man is to be strong as men go, to be a strong woman is to be strong as women go, and are there not feats of strength which men can perform and not women? But this consideration will go by the board if the property (truly) predicated of this man and this woman in calling them both 'strong' is viewed as their common property. For what possible grounds could there then be for saying that it was not the same in both?

We might say that language, by allowing the formation of abstract nouns that 'correspond' to predicates – nouns such as 'redness', 'brightness', 'health', 'strength' and innumerable others – lends itself to the fiction that words from the logician's formal vocabulary are signs for concepts amongst others. For it is not for nothing that we call such abstract nouns 'names of properties (qualities)', since, unlike expressions of the form 'the property of being F', they display some of the versatility of proper names, attracting to themselves a variety of predicates, relational and non-relational. The advantage of augmenting our vocabulary in this way is obvious: we achieve thereby an economy of expression so that, for instance, 'She admires strength in men' does duty for 'She admires strong men in that they are strong'. But if we say with Socrates, 'In its character as strength, strength is the same in man and woman', or with Russell, 'Things are white because they have the quality of whiteness', we are handling the abstract nouns as if the fiction were reality – as if the description 'names of qualities' defined a class of expressions by citing a concept under which anything had to fall to be named by a member of that class. And this leads straight to paradox in the cases of abstract nouns corresponding to what have been called attributive, as opposed to predicative, adjectives. For whilst 'This infant is strong' does not admit of the analysis

'This human being is an infant and this human being is strong', the equivalent proposition 'This infant has the quality of strength' *will* admit of the analysis 'This human being is an infant and this human being has the quality of strength'. That is to say, it will admit of this analysis on the theory of universals, where it asserts a relation between an individual and a property, just as 'This infant has measles' admits of the analysis 'This human being is an infant and this human being has measles'.

Notes

Logical form and hypothetical reasoning

1 Wittgenstein (1961) at 3.327: 'A sign does not determine a logical form unless it is taken together with its logico-syntactical employment.'

2 Sanford (1989) p. 226, seeks to show that whilst there are valid contrapositions, there is no valid *form* of argument by contraposition, adducing 'If I draw a flush, I will not draw a straight flush. Therefore if I draw a straight flush, I will not draw a flush' as an example of an invalid contraposition. But here one can only reply that if the inference is unsound, that only shows that what is contraposed is no hypothetical. And indeed it seems clear that the premiss is a concessive statement, with 'if' meaning 'even if'. How else is it to be understood?

3 For the notion of a performative verb, *vide* Austin (1962).

4 Thus Sanford (1989) p. 225, cites 'If Smith dies before the election, Jones will win the election. If Jones wins the election, Smith will retire after the election. Therefore, if Smith dies before the election, Smith will retire after the election' as an example of an invalid hypothetical syllogism, when neither premisses nor conclusion are of the form *If p, q*.

5 Von Wright (1957) p. 131. With which we may compare Quine (1952) p. 12, where he writes 'An affirmation of the form "if p, then q" is commonly felt less as an affirmation of a conditional than as a conditional affirmation of the consequent'.

6 Moore (1922) p. 291.

7 This useful term is borrowed from Wittgenstein (1961), where it is introduced at 5.101.

8 Quine (1952) p. 15. The statements he is seeking to account for he calls 'conditionals'.

9 *Begriffsschrift* §5, in van Heijenoort (1970) p. 14.

10 Compare the following:

> 'Either the butler or the gardener did it. Therefore if the butler didn't do it, the gardener did.' This piece of reasoning ... may seem tedious, but it is surely compelling. Yet if it is a valid inference, then the indicative conditional conclusion must be logically equivalent to the truth-functional material conditional, and *this* conclusion has consequences that are notoriously paradoxical.
> (From 'Indicative Conditionals' by Robert Stalnaker, *Philosophia*, 5, 1975, reprinted in Harper, Stalnaker and Pearce (1981) pp. 193–210).

11 Frege (1979) p. 198. The present translation, which is slightly different from the one in the text, is to be preferred.

12 Frege (1959) Introduction p. x.
13 Wittgenstein (1967a) §22.
14 Wittgenstein (1961) 3.143.
15 It is at best misleading to represent Frege as holding that a sentence is a complex name. If a formation beginning with the assertion sign does not designate anything, as Frege is careful to point out – *vide* Frege (1960) footnote p. 34 – then neither does the corresponding sentence of ordinary language, whose Mood is not conveyed by an element within the sentence.
16 Wittgenstein (1961). The German is 'räumlich', which Pears and McGuinness render as 'spatial', but 'three-dimensional' is to be preferred. Do not written signs count as spatial objects?
17 Thus what has been called the *logical problem of conditionals*, which is described by Stalnaker as 'the task of describing the formal properties of the *conditional function*: a function usually represented in English by the words "if . . . then", taking ordered pairs of propositions into propositions', does not exist. The elements of grammar show that there is no such function and you start off on the wrong foot if you begin an enquiry into hypotheticals, as writers commonly do, with the assumption that the conjunction forming a hypothetical defines a function taking propositions into propositions, whether a truth-function or not. As we see, its role is not commensurate with that of such a conjunction. The quotation is from 'A Theory of Conditionals', in Harper, Stalnaker and Pearce (1981) pp. 41–55.
18 *Begriffsschrift* §17, in van Heijenoort (1970) p. 44. Frege refers to the principle as 'the judgement that justifies the transition from *modus ponens* to *modus tollens*'.
19 Carroll (1894).
20 A set of natural deduction rules for (classical) propositional and predicate logic is to be found in Lemmon (1965). For Gentzen's own account of this form of reasoning see Gentzen (1964).
21 *Begriffsschrift* §17 and §18, in van Heijenoort (1970) pp. 44–5.
22 Wittgenstein (1961) 6.1262 and 6.1263.
23 Wittgenstein (1967b) §679.
24 Quine (1952) pp. 14–15. To be what Quine calls 'contrafactual' it seems that a hypothetical has both to be non-indicative in form and have a false antecedent. As we have seen, these conditions are independent of one another.
25 Lewis (1986) p. 43.
26 The argument and example are from Van McGee (1985). The author takes the statement 'If that creature is a fish then if it has lungs then it is a lung fish' to have only one antecedent, hence the title of his paper.

Formal relations

1 Frege (1960) pp. 54–5.
2 Bradley (1902) p. 33.
3 Waismann (1967) p. 251.
4 Ibid. p. 252.
5 Wittgenstein (1974) pp. 199–201.

Universals: logic and metaphor

1 Russell (1943) p. 95.
2 Ibid. p. 98.
3 Bradley (1902) pp. 32–3. Because we have cited Bradley only to illustrate how the

construction 'The relation R relates ...' gets deployed relationally, with the puzzlement this gives rise to, we have neglected the fact – which Russell seems to overlook – that Bradley's polemic against relations assumes the form of a dilemma of which the argument by regress is the first horn.

4 Russell (1927) pp. 263–4.
5 Frege (1979) p. 177. To adapt Frege's remark to my terminology, I have replaced throughout his 'concept' by my 'property'. This does not misrepresent the point he is making.
6 Plato (1956) pp. 117–18.

Bibliography

Austin, J. L. (1962) *How To Do Things With Words*, Oxford: Oxford University Press.

Bradley, F. H. (1902) *Appearance and Reality*, 2nd edn, Oxford: Oxford University Press.

Carroll, L. (1894) 'A Logical Paradox', *Mind* N. S. No. 11, Edinburgh.

Frege, G. (1959) *The Foundations of Arithmetic*, translated by J. L. Austin, Oxford: Basil Blackwell.

Frege, G. (1960) *Translations from the Philosophical Writings of Gottlob Frege*, edited by P. T. Geach and M. Black, Oxford: Basil Blackwell.

Frege, G. (1979) *Posthumous Writings*, translated by Peter Long and Roger White, Oxford: Basil Blackwell.

Gentzen, G. (1964) 'Investigations into Logical Deduction', translated by M. E. Szabo, *American Philosophical Quarterly*, October 1964.

Harper, W. L., Stalnaker, R. and Pearce, G. (eds) (1981) *Ifs*, Dordrecht, Holland: D. Reidel Publishing Co.

Lemmon, E. J. (1965) *Beginning Logic*, Walton-on-Thames, Surrey: Nelson.

Lewis, David (1986) *Counterfactuals*, Oxford: Basil Blackwell.

Moore, G. E. (1922) *Philosophical Studies*, London: Kegan Paul, Trench, Trubner & Co. Ltd.

Plato (1956) *Protagoras and Meno*, translated by W. K. C. Guthrie, Harmondsworth: Penguin Books.

Quine, W. V. (1952) *Methods of Logic*, London: Routledge & Kegan Paul.

Russell, B. (1927) *An Outline of Philosophy*, London: George Allen & Unwin.

Russell, B. (1943) *The Problems of Philosophy*, Oxford: Oxford University Press.

Sanford, D. H. (1989) *If P, then Q*, London and New York: Routledge.

van Heijenoort, Jean (ed.) (1970) *From Frege to Gödel*, Cambridge, Mass.: Harvard University Press.

Van McGee (1985) 'A Counterexample to Modus Ponens', *Journal of Philosophy*, LXXXII, 9, September 1985.

von Wright, G. H. (1957) *Logical Studies*, London: Routledge & Kegan Paul.

Waismann, F. (1967), *Wittgenstein und der Weiner Kreis*, Oxford: Basil Blackwell.

Wittgenstein, L. (1961) *Tractatus Logico-Philosophicus*, translated by D. F. Pears and B. F. McGuinness, London: Routledge & Kegan Paul.

Wittgenstein, L. (1967a) *Philosophical Investigations*, Oxford: Basil Blackwell.

Wittgenstein, L. (1967b) *Zettel*, Oxford: Basil Blackwell.

Wittgenstein, L. (1974) *Philosophical Grammar*, Oxford: Basil Blackwell.

Printed in the United States
by Baker & Taylor Publisher Services